Custom Reality
and You

PETER COFFIN

ACKNOWLEDGEMENTS

A massive thanks must go to everyone who made this book even remotely possible. To my patrons, whose support is utterly vital to have the time to do this. To friends who have listened to endless rambling and offered feedback. To Penelope Iremonger, a gracious and detail-oriented editor who brought the book up several notches on the dial, as well as Oliver Thorne for the extremely helpful notes. To my parents, Joe and Carol, for raising me to think critically and for their love. To my children, Harrison and Gemma, for making it very hard to write a book, but being great sources of joy and inspiration. Finally, thank you to my beautiful wife and partner, Ashleigh, for your intellect, your conversation, your time, your love, and your patience. ♥

CONTENTS

1. INTRODUCTION

Either I was an artistic genius, or my art teacher was a bit lazy. My money is on the latter. Older teachers tend to come from a tougher time, or at the very least, view themselves as such. They may have lived through Vietnam or a World War, and they may have even directly dealt with the horrors of those conflicts. I can't say I've experienced anything like that, though there are young people who have, but it seems like they would be hell. Teachers that either directly or indirectly saw hell were more likely to be tougher on students.

Though my art teacher was old, she went pretty soft on us. She also really liked Picasso. People only needed about a third of the time she would allot to complete a project and when we were done, we were allowed to do just about whatever we wanted until the deadline. She was a nice person and very encouraging to everyone. I would say it was a good experience for me. A light workload and a legitimately supportive teacher make for a class made up mostly of students who don't rush and actually try to do well.

I had art in my second class period of the day, after homeroom/advisory/whatever your generation calls it. So, if I was not working on a project in my second hour, I had two hours to not think that hard. Which is good, because I was often up until 4am playing video games, which isn't smart but is relatable!

Anyways, I had an hour to take it *very* easy followed by an hour to take it *pretty* easy. At this point you should probably discard the possibility that I am an artistic genius. I wasn't then and I'm not now. It was at least a fun class, though.

If 9/11 hadn't happened while I was in art class, that would be all there is to my memory of it.

To be clear, the first plane hit about fifteen minutes before second period art. They had a TV set up before 9am, though, when class started. Upon walking in a minute or two before class officially started, I didn't understand what was on the screen. By 9:03am, more students were in the classroom than were supposed to be. They'd been filing in because it was one of the only classrooms with a television, and it was very clear something very big was happening.

The next fifteen minutes of the broadcast were intense. The channel we were watching had a close-up of the first tower burning when the second plane hit at 9:03. So, we didn't actually see it live, but the anchors were narrating the scene. The one talking kind of trailed off and the other let out an "oh my God!" After a moment of regaining composure, they noted there was what appeared to be another plane hitting the second tower.

Another fifteen minutes passed and it was 2003. We all aged about two years in that fifteen minutes, and I was no longer in art class. I was starting a program at the local community college that would last just a bit less than twelve minutes before I dropped out. Another war in Iraq was underway and health savings accounts were the hip new thing. Everything was totally normal. For sure.

Not so much. To many of us, reality was changing, fracturing further beyond the borders of its latest traumatic wound. Personally, that fracture lead me to heavily question my role as someone shortly entering adulthood in America. What was "the American Dream?" Why do these people hate us? We're just normal people living our lives… What did we do to them? It made no sense to me, and for good reason. I didn't understand reality.

I wasn't the only one. From the liberals torn between capital and their own morals to the conspiracy theorists, reality was behaving like a cracked windshield that you don't get replaced because you can *definitely still see!*

In any case, it's 2018 and we're still taking the side roads to avoid getting a fine. This doesn't work forever, though. We've gotten one before and with many broken reality windshields. We've caved and replaced it more than once. This particular windshield had been mostly intact for several generations, though, and we were beginning to think that would be the one that protected the inside of our car from the friction of moving air forever.

9/11 changed each of our individual realities in different was, and cemented the Middle East as an ongoing topic of discussion for reasons (I can say that, I'm a millennial). I want to quickly summarize a principle that has, mostly outside the view of our everyday lives, driven a large fraction of the sweeping changes in the 20th century:

If you have oil, we will come democratize your ass with some serious freedom. That's the military reality.

To accomplish this, the United States Armed Forces employ a wide variety of weapons. Some of them are autonomous, while others are piloted by kids in a military arcade where they get medals and PTSD, instead of tickets and pizza. One can't trade them in for prizes, either, and will constantly remember how one killed some people at a wedding when you try to sleep.

Do you ever think about this stuff? Doesn't it bother you that what I am describing is not even something anyone would dispute? Did it feel normal? Did it feel real?

I mean, aside from the arcade imagery. I am more than willing to acknowledge there aren't a lot of arcades anymore, but I thought it made my point pretty well. Not everyone has read Ender's Game, though that would have worked, too. The way we frame information changes the way we interpret it, which is something I want you to heavily consider as you read.

Not just this book. Anytime you read.

In January of 1996, someone said "Google is a great name for a company" and filed the paperwork. Almost 20 years later, they realized it was a bad idea and changed it to "Alphabet," which is… I guess a less bad name. Anyways, the company created an unprecedented search engine that I won't try to make sound cool because it's a search engine. It was still quite impressive, though. Instead of ranking pages based on the number of times it mentioned keywords (as its competitors did), it checked the amount of times a website was linked elsewhere.

That is to say, if you searched "butt," it figured out how many times pages containing the word "butt" linked to each other and ordered the results based on this. If something got linked to more, it was more likely to be useful. In theory, this discouraged gaming the system. Previously, by simply making a page with nothing but 100,000 instances of the word "butt," that page would be determined relevant to the word "butt." But checking backlink volume supposedly discouraged tag loading and required a page to be connected elsewhere to be relevant. You supposedly couldn't control how many other pages linked to you. *Challenge Accepted.*

People figured out that if they made multiple websites all over the place linking to the website they want to rank, it would rank. Google kept trying to develop new ways to rank that were less easy to manipulate, but in the end people always manipulated them. People like the idea of ranking well; it's how you win. Winning is supposedly important in life, and you can't win if you don't play.

However, when you play the game in a way the game makers don't expect or appreciate, they tend to create rules to stop it. In a vast, anonymous, unregulatable expanse of virtual space, it's kind of hard to enforce rules and people don't care much for them anyway. In fact, that was a lot of the point of the internet.

So instead, game makers must build systems that create the result they want. Now, if I told you I knew everything about how Google ranks pages after many years of conflict and observation, I would be telling you a lie. I do, however, know that there are three words that sum up the result that scares me the most: "best for you."

What is best for you? What exactly does that term mean? Does it mean something that helps you? Does it mean what keeps you healthy or expands your mind?

Does it mean something that fits your taste? Does it apply to everything you search or just some things? Does telling you what is "best for you" mean withholding other information that might contradict it? Could that other information be true? Does that mean "best for you" might be false? Could they both be true? Is it mutually exclusive? Are algorithms the only thing that do this?

When you became an adult, there were probably things you ended up believing that contradict the ones you were raised on. You may have been raised Catholic and become an atheist. Hell, you may have become a Mormon. The environment we're socialized in is our built-in social network. Just like the social networks created and maintained by massive corporations we all spend our days on, it curates reality for us.

For instance, it is not terribly difficult to see that both Fox News and CNN are simply different interpretations of the same things much of the time. Both selectively withhold information to make the assertions they do, and they cater to the lifestyle the viewer perceives themselves to be.

As a quick warning, one of the following two paragraphs is going to make most Americans reading this book uncomfortable or angry.

Someone who watches Fox News considers themselves conservative; they perceive themselves to be traditional and Very Rational™, meaning they believe that their decisions are not influenced by emotions. The set of facts *that were fact* in 1950 are the foundation of a healthy life in these people's opinions, meaning they're still influenced by certain ideas. For instance, the Red Scare their parents were terrified of. They might understand somewhere in the depths of their minds that the world has moved on from that point, but rather than acknowledge this as development, they tend to believe that the world has lost its way. They think we need to go back to The Good Old Days™ and whether they know it or not, that usually makes them bigots or unwitting accomplices to bigots.

Someone who watches CNN or MSNBC probably considers themselves "liberal." They consider this specifically to mean "the opposite of a conservative," despite the fact that other than the evangelicals and ethno-nationalists who have injected their views into conservatism, both conservatism and what a lot of Americans call "liberalism" are founded in liberalism. What we call liberalism is center-right to center-left. This person believes themselves to be socially tolerant, but won't admit to themselves that our country is built on a power structure that exacerbates inequality and other problems they think can be just solved by getting people to accept the idea that they need to talk nicer. They're sanctimonious, they believe in an elite but they don't call it that, and they think they really like science. What they actually like, either consciously or not, is the idea that their choices make them better than other people. They also believe they should be rewarded for it.

Liberals and conservatives are both weirdly enamored with advancing the interests of a free market, though liberals are pretty sure that they aren't. Well, at least the liberals who aren't in power aren't. You'll be amazed at how much this little piece of information matters in explaining what has happened to reality.

The rift between these two demographics is both huge and tiny. That sentence seems counterintuitive, but later, you'll be able to come back to this part and say "oh, that is actually true." It requires at least a few new concepts, too. I had to make up some new terms and phrases for any of it to make sense, though, which I think was worth the years I've put into these ideas. I get to name the ideas that ended the world. That's badass!

That's an intentionally dramatic statement; obviously, we are all still here. But what is "here?" What exactly are we talking about when we say "reality?" How "postmodern" is this book and how much of an existential crisis is it going to cause?

The manipulation of reality didn't start with the World Trade Center's falling. It also didn't start with algorithms or social networks. These things enabled it on pretty high levels over the last decade, but reality has been on this trajectory for centuries. We could spend a long time in this intro setting up historical context to give you a fuller view, but from this point I'll reserve further contextualization for when talking specific mechanics or situations.

Please remember that my concepts of how this works are based mostly in observation. I'm attempting to create and apply framing devices that can both explain and aide in further criticism and observation of the "reality crisis" this world is currently having. I also want to remind you that this isn't new; profit was always nudging people in this direction.

Also, "Reality Crisis" is apparently also a Japanese metal band. Google told me that.

So, what is "custom reality?" I think this term is basically the simplest version of the thing I want to say. Perhaps people may already say it, too. I don't know, but I don't hear a lot of people saying things like "individualized reality" or "cultivated identity." These are terms I made up and for that reason, they are not "real." Yet.

There aren't a lot of ongoing conversations about lifestyle marketing's deep effect on our lives, nor are there many that characterize it as I intend to. Typically, the mainstream understanding of lifestyle marketing might influence what brand of soap you may buy, or whether you drink only Coke or Pepsi and do so with fierce loyalty, despite these products' similarity.

Why you may like Coke or Pepsi has no relation to why you're a Republican or Democrat… right? Directly speaking, probably not. But the methodology behind brand differentiation, lifestyle marketing, and political loyalty aren't that different.

Custom reality isn't just the result of marketing, though. There is a load of factors: the ideals of the United States of America. I'm going to say some stuff about how individualism is not actually leading us towards a collective reality. I'm not going to tell you that there should be no such thing as an individual or that we need to stop acting as individuals with their own identities. I am going to tell you that individualism is a means to be directed by manipulation of the environment we are presented with.

A lot of people spend time talking about how stupid everyone is, how there's an Idiocracy forming, how the idiot majority is screwing everything up for us, and any number of infinite variations on how 90% of people are stupid and 10% of people are constantly trying to fix the world for them. To drop the first curse word of the book, I think that's horseshit.

People make rational decisions based on the world presented to them. I'm not saying that genuinely makes their decisions rational, so don't you dare think that. Keep in mind that the goal is to understand and not to excuse. People who are ignorant about things often are that way because they've never been exposed to an argument that's not condescending.

Unfortunately, a sympathetic ear is often attached to a mouth that wants something. This mouth and ear combo is also often attached to someone inherently closer to the sensibilities of the person in need of the ear than someone who might want to attempt to convince them of opposing points, like a family member or friend.

Through familial, social, analog and digital conduits, we have the mechanisms for creating a custom reality from parts given to us selectively. We aren't sheep. Every one of us is a shepherd. We are all leaders, thinking for ourselves, making our own decisions. That might sound positive, but it's not. Eventually, we must realize that we're at one end of a hallway and our decision is limited to staying there or walking to the other end. We are free to choose whichever end of a rectangle we want to occupy. Woo.

Essentially, we aren't tricked at all. We're allowed a decent amount of agency, but it only works in a world with very limited choice. Therefore, it isn't power in the real world but instead in a virtual one. We are living in a custom reality—a dream world. While we occupy our individualized existence, our essence is easy to control.

Sounds like a fun book!

PETER COFFIN

2. QUESTIONING WHAT'S REAL

I'll ask you a question that's been made obvious by the title of this chapter: have you ever questioned reality? Of course you have. A cat would probably do the same if it was smart enough. Because we're such big smarties, like cats, asking *super intense* questions about the world around us is inevitable.

Cats, however, cannot ask those questions because they cannot talk. Well, unless you consider "Oh my dog, oh long John, oh long Johnson, oh Don piano, why I eyes ya, all the livelong day" to be more than nonsense. Further, cats cannot read. They also poop in a box, like, that's not weird?

It's weird.

If you asked a cat about postmodernism, that cat would probably look at you as if to say, "I shit in a box."

Starting conversations about the current state of facts will often steer itself toward a discussion on postmodernism, usually negatively. There are a few people who repeatedly call themselves "skeptics," both in traditional and new media, who you may see reference postmodernism in a negative context. These clowns tend to paint it as the reason nothing is "real" anymore, which reveals a flawed understanding of what postmodernism is.

Despite what you'll hear any number of cartoon animals in tuxedos say if you search "postmodernism" on YouTube, the actual underlying philosophy is not "everyone gets to define their own personal truth." It's a philosophical approach that questions human perspective; it is acknowledgement of the flaws in our perception. There was a broad movement of philosophers and artists who used this approach to deconstruct cultural norms, evaluate them, and attempt to ascertain their validity. To simplify (a lot), it's skepticism by another word.

In fact, most philosophical methodology is. Postmodernism just happens to be the one that was skeptical of the objective aspects of modernism. Which is very good, because though modernism brought us to societally accept more self-awareness through its skepticism of the Age of Enlightenment's sureness in its collective conclusions, it was overzealous in its utilitarianism. Modernist conclusion, just like the Age of Enlightenment and other philosophical development before it, regarded itself as objective or provable. But every new wave of philosophical thinking usually regards itself as the final form; believing we've reached peak enlightenment doesn't give much in way of understanding who we all are as different people. Postmodern philosophers broke the link in that chain.

What we might call the "postmodern approach" is what led to the so-called "skeptic" cultural movement that gained prominence during the last decade or so. This is neither a good thing nor a bad thing, despite all the pretend skeptics definitely being a bad thing. It also yielded social sciences, aided in the development of today's feminism, and in *your* questioning of movies, music, news, art, architecture, or just about everything. We were raised to deconstruct; it's *damn* good framing for the stage of critical thinking in which we ascertain base level assumptions. We really could do with more acknowledgement and acceptance of our inherent lack of perfection. None of us are gods.

A cartoon animal in a tuxedo on YouTube will not tell you that. A cat might. Also, because a cat is probably not masculine enough for the kind of skeptic that makes those kinds of videos, the cartoon tuxedo animal won't be a cat.

My understanding of postmodernism is derived mainly from some of Michel Foucault's critical histories and the work of his contemporaries, but I don't intend to force their material upon you. *You have a life*, let's take a TL;DR ("too long; didn't read," for less internet-y folks) perspective on the specifics and then talk more about how these ideas slot into society.

Postmodernism is characterized by its questioning of objective truth, which is a good thing to be questioning. When one criticizes something using a postmodern approach, one deconstructs the elements of an assertion or observation to reach a base level understanding from which to find truth. It's not mere simplification; deconstruction means analyzing context, connections, implications, consequences, materials, and motivations, among other things. Obviously, that doesn't include screaming that "nothing is real" at passers-by from an alley while on a three-day binge, inexplicably wearing a stolen Technicolor Dreamcoat. It does, however, require you to understand that "reality" and "fact" are *products of human perception.*

"Reality" is a word. There was no concept of reality before humans came into existence, in no small part because there was no concept *of a concept* before humans came into existence. Words didn't exist before they came out of people's mouths.

Everything we observe is automatically viewed through the lens of perspective, seen differently due to variations in everything from our optic nerves to our cultural sensibilities. There is no such thing as someone who observes something with no perspective whatsoever, and because of this, there is no such thing as objectivity.

For instance, there are a select few of us who just despise the internet's thing for pictures of cats. *I am one of those people.* Yeah, I said it. *Come at me, bro.*

You may have thought it to be an objective fact that cat pictures on the internet is the best thing for a bad day, but guess what? I don't. In fact, they genuinely make me feel *worse.* Getting cat photos sent to me when I'm down makes me feel like I'm on a path I can't change, so the best I can do is distract myself. It makes me feel as if my efforts are futile and sends me on a path to a darker place. For some people, it's *medicine* that is the best thing for a bad day. For others, it's sex, drugs, chess, a good joke or driving around in the rain with the orchestral versions of '90s Japanese role-playing game soundtracks on loop. I don't know!

I just know that if I'm feeling down, Caturday puts me in a worse place than I was before the feline love-bombing. Though, I do very much like cats. I also know that this is not a relatable statement. But nothing is objective because no one is objective. This is partly why we value sympathy and empathy so much; the idea that one might understand or even have parallel emotions helps overcome the total lack of objectivity in a human world. The imperfection goes much further, though.

Memory provides us with a good idea as to how imperfect human perception modifies perspective continually over time. Yadin Dudai, a Professor of Neurobiology at the Weizmann Institute of Science of Rehovot, Israel, put together a collection of essays on how memory works called "Memory from A to Z: Keywords, Concepts, and Beyond" that I'll attempt to summarize my understanding of here:

Human memory is an extremely complicated construct; it doesn't operate digitally like a data storage device, nor does a memory exist singularly. It exists as an index of many sensory events which are "stored" (for lack of a

better word) all over the place. Where you mi
memory exists as "event.mem," it's more like
and "event.ear" floating somewhere in a neural netwo..,
encoded through the strengthening and weakening of
synaptic connections. Whereas data is stored in ones and
zeros, human memory is stored in a much more analog
manner.

The next thing one needs to know about memory is
that every recollection of it acts as a new event. As one
recalls something, the parts of the brain that handle the
different sensory functions act as if they are experiencing it
again. We also have maintenance recollections which take
place specifically to preserve a memory instead of allowing
it to weaken, but any form of recollection needs to be
regarded as a new event. This in mind, recollection is
essentially rewriting a memory, possibly because organic
matter is never in a permanent state.

In this mode of preservation, we must acknowledge a
specific weakness: an imperfect mold creates imperfect
casts.

Your memory is you. If we didn't have memories, we
would not have identity. This means identity itself is
imperfect, as is everything humans have come up with.
"Fact," however, is something that someone defined in
short-term memory, or possibly even considered a long
time, then committed it to paper, papyrus, or cave wall. We
mostly agree on what "fact" is supposed to mean, but that
doesn't mean we agree on what "facts" are.

If something is created by (or is in some other way the
product of) humans, it is imperfect. We cannot claim our
observations to be universal. It is self-aggrandizement to
call our perception anything other than imperfect.
Evidence is imperfect, and must be accepted for it to
matter. The processes we use to accept evidence are
imperfect, for the evidence passes through the eyeballs and
memories of those examining it. The person perceiving it
has had a very specific life experience and that colors their

interpretation, as well. The idea of "true or false" is imperfect, and we must understand our own implicit biases cannot be avoided.

The only thing a human could objectively state about "fact" is that it is not objective. I am joking (mostly).

Yes, there is most certainly a universal commonality outside of human perception. The universe is as it is, whether we are here or not. However, truth is a concept invented by humanity, just as facts are, and all other words. Not only is our perception of reality colored by our own perspective, but so is our recollection. Our memory, the way that we retain a grip on reality, is astoundingly imperfect as well.

Memory is not definite, and nor is the person with the most photographic memory in existence perfect. Memory is analog and in flux; it is fluid and in every way unlike how computers store data. It's also not persistent. The ink on the pages of a book doesn't change every time you read it; memory does.

Not only is perception imperfect, but your ability to go back to that perception is imperfect. Therefore, your perception of facts and reality cannot be called objective. Because it's not.

This was a typical assertion of postmodern philosophers. For instance, Michel Foucault presented his ideas and theories on modernism as a critical history of various subjects. This is a simplification, but modernism presented an objective truth and objective reality. My assertion, as well as anyone who puts any stock at all in postmodernism, is that perspective makes that impossible. This isn't to say we should all just live in our own little bubbles; we must acknowledge historical and cultural concepts on which we power our societies. But ongoing criticism must continue. We must be skeptical of everything, but only if we understand all the historical and cultural contexts, as well as its implications.

So basically, like YouTube skeptics, but with information and acknowledgment of culture. For the uninitiated, "skepticism" on YouTube is anything but, functioning primarily as a kind of resistance to progressive critique of social and economic norms.

Our perceived certainties close us off from what is certain. The universe is cold and unfeeling, but our perception of it is colored by, if not entirely a result of, our biological imperfection and our life experience. It's both nature and nurture that we can't perceive objectively, and postmodernism is one of many means to acknowledge and criticize our bias. It exists because modernists believed that science was somehow perfect, and that humanity was able to be objective.

I believe postmodernism's net effect was simply reminding us that we aren't perfect.

There is a flaw in it, though; it doesn't go much further than that. We use it to deconstruct and analyze our society's norms, and those who subscribe to the approach often follow that same process when philosophically critiquing things. This results in many people effectively bungee jumping alone regarding critical thought. No one is there to pull them in, so they must do it themselves.

This creates a rabbit hole. If you get lost in it, deconstruction can waste away all meaning around you. Sure, if nothing means anything, nothing hurts. Just the same, nothing feels good. The world around us can appear to be ridiculous in the most depressing of ways. If the only thing we do is deconstruct, we can strip away meaning and become very nihilistic, and not the careful, positive nihilism some have created through personal meaning. I'm talking the Markus "Notch" Persson kind of nihilism.

Similarly, one can use postmodern deconstruction to find a sweet spot for exploitation. One can profit, either socially or economically, by taking things down to their base and applying their findings to an agenda. This isn't postmodernism; it just started there. In much the same way, Adolf Hitler was once an innocent child who played with toys and shat his pants.

On the 22nd of January 2017, Kellyanne Conway, senior advisor in Donald Trump's White House, appeared on the NBC's *Meet the Press* and in defense of their press secretary's loose handling of numbers said, "You're saying it's a falsehood. and Sean Spicer… gave alternative facts to that."

Kellyanne Conway likely utilized something akin to postmodern deconstruction to break down the societal concept of fact. I don't know that she would describe her approach as such and it's quite possible she doesn't know anything about it, but "alternative fact" is an idea that started there.

"Alternative fact" doesn't justify; it *defines*. The term is not just some excuse to say things that aren't true; it reflects an actual phenomenon. Donald Trump is hardly the first person to say things that don't reflect our broad social truth in order to muddy the waters. This is a popular tactic that more than a few "real" politicians, and significantly more everyday folks, regularly employ. Many believe themselves when they say these things, too.

On December 5th, 2013, 95-year-old Nelson Mandela died after suffering from a prolonged respiratory infection. However, many people think he died in prison in 1988. The likely reason for this is that it was announced he had tuberculosis while imprisoned in 1988. Several times since then, his death has been announced or talked about, including by former President George H.W. Bush. More than one book claims he died in 1988, 1991, and so on. There is a collective misremembering of the death of Nelson Mandela.

What is known as The Mandela Effect is all the proof you'll ever need that reality has been individualized. It originated from skepticism of mainstream narratives and, in truth, it comes from a healthy place. The conclusion goes beyond deconstruction, though; it's a repeated mistake by a lot of individuals, reinforced by other individuals. This situation brought itself about through misinformation (both intentional and unintentional) and is regarded by some as proof that people are living in different dimensional timelines.

A lot of people define The Mandela Effect as a set of parallel universes clashing and changing our memories or some such horseshit. Anyone familiar with memes ("viral content" for the lay) can pretty easily figure out how The Mandela Effect works: stuff gets popular and then *purple monkey dishwasher*. Now, neither "stuff" nor "popular" have anything about being factual baked into their definitions; misremembering happens whether erroneous accounts of an event become popular or not. People accept them as valid, no matter how bizarre.

I believe people make this mistake for the same reasons they join multi-level marketing schemes: a lot of the time, verifiable information is negative, disappointing, and/or delivered in a condescending or elitist manner. Also, a person claiming to be an authority rubs many of us the wrong way, as we're repeatedly asked to be their own authority on everything. You've likely heard a variant of the phrase "we've represented all sides, now it's up to the viewer to decide for themselves!" That's validation by deferment; apparently, we're supposed to conclude that a multinational corporation doesn't have the resources to look into something and it's up to us, the rational outsider, to find the *real* truth.

When questionable conclusions are reached by an attitude of skepticism and distrust toward popular narratives and ideologies, it's both because our methods are individualized and how they become further so. Our counter-arguments may be rooted in fallacious logic or traditional thinking when we accept validation without verification. But because we got there of our own volition, we think it's correct, regardless of where we came from. In thinking this, we may deconstruct things down to a base level, but our own biases fill in the blanks rather than insight.

When Kellyanne Conway used the term "alternative facts," it was perhaps a new phrase; it was certainly the first I'd heard of it. It was also a perverted testimony to just how far the deconstruction of "objective fact" has come. But neither the impetus or result is "postmodernism." It takes more to erode reality than simply questioning it.

American life, in its endless stream of conditioning, has been priming us to believe that whatever we choose to consume, we're empowered for having chosen. This is much more related to the idea of "my reality."

Media has not done much to help. I didn't mention "we've shown both sides, now it's up to the viewer to decide" for no reason. Media happily represents every issue as a two-sided one, including issues that have long since been verified or debunked through evidence-based methods. We are given the basics, but we are left to decide for ourselves. We are the leader presented with the briefing. We're asked to make the decision where to take our own personal Nation of One™.

Why is it a problem to represent assertions that have been debunked as valid opinions? Tell me this: when Robert De Niro says "what, you don't think we should worry about vaccine safety" is he *not* trying to undermine conclusions that have seen rigorous scrutiny through usage of fallacious logic presented as common sense? Does his status as a beloved actor and member of the film community lend credence to his assertions? Should it?

Yet, some people listen to him, and they do it for a complex set of reasons. Maybe they're a fan. Maybe they aren't but regard him as high in status or wealthy enough to simply know more than we small folk. Maybe people assume he doesn't make decisions without expert input. He certainly has better access to information and the people who research it than those of us without much material wealth, so assuming he uses that access isn't terribly absurd (despite being incorrect).

A person could even just have an underlying distrust for the medical profession due to an incident at some point in their own lives. These aren't illogical; there's more than a few people with more than a few reasons to feel as if they've been wronged by a doctor.

For instance, the most recent US Transgender Survey reports a whopping 33% of transgender people, who saw a healthcare provider in the past year, having at least one negative experience specifically related to being transgender, with even higher rates for people of color and those with disabilities. That's an extremely high rate; imagine if your experience with doctors was "at least one out of three are going to fuck with my day."

The information De Niro has disseminated regarding vaccines ranges from "provably false" to "just asking questions" depending on who he's speaking with. Giving him a platform to speak about vaccines as some kind of expert creates a dynamic where he's deemed credible, though. You may not consider him to be and I certainly don't, but if he's presented as an authority, it undermines an actual specialist on a topic and in more than one way. The effect of perspective should become obvious here.

If there were a panel of (or a debate between) specialists, and if Robert De Niro is part of it, he will automatically appear to be on equal footing with doctors, researchers, and various professionals who back up their assertions with something more than conjecture. He *isn't*, though, because the actual specialists here used scientific methodology to conclude what they have. De Niro has experienced personal hardship and, perhaps, has gotten a lot of unsatisfying answers.

I get why that might lead someone on a path to alternative ideas, but when those ideas come from a debunked study an insurance company commissioned for a lawsuit with results that can't be duplicated (and got its head researcher's medical license revoked), it might be time to ask the question if De Niro is genuinely "just asking questions."

Now, whenever someone becomes anti-vaccine after their kid's learning disability manifests, I sympathize. Life deviated from the plan; things didn't go how they imagined. The fantasy is not the reality. However, I can't help wondering whether many of these parents view their children as an individual with unique challenges or if they see them as a broken promise from their maker. That's not to say I think these parents don't love their children. I, however, rarely read a message board post, a professional article, or a tweet that isn't all about what *the parents* "deal with."

My belief isn't that the onus is on them, though. Those who understand the benefits of planting seeds of distrust in parents who are desperate for answers, creating new markets full of products and services, are the ones who did this. There's plenty of incentive to find people with that need and attempt to "inform" them.

Anti-vaccination is a *hard* position to take. There's built-in alienation that can only come from having a perspective that society just doesn't accept its validity.

With the escalating pressure to constantly be perfect, it makes sense that a person who has gone for decades without a release might finally metaphysically explode.

The obvious intent on catering to a specific audience through the selective omission of facts has made people suspicious of ostensibly true information due to *who presented it.* This has led many to alternative media outlets cropping up. However, these outlets aren't usually offering a collective, evidence-oriented substitute on the narrative-oriented mainstream media. They're just offering a near-infinite number of counter-narratives. And ads.

Between broad, partisan-driven mainstream narratives and narrow, fragmented, confirmation bias-oriented alternative narratives, there's a start point and a rabbit hole for nearly any assertion you can make. There's content that can confirm anything you want to think, because it's profitable to co-opt your deconstruction of something of which you're right to be skeptical. Making facts into a personalized, "choose your own adventure" sort of affair is a brilliant means of control because those operating with the means present the choices.

With all this in mind, it's important to note specifically that I think deconstruction of universalism and realism has been a good thing. It is utterly impossible to describe any of this without it. An imperfect, human approach cannot yield unquestionable truth. Yet universalism and realism (approaches created by humanity) *purport to* do so. Among those truths are religion, and not the "found God, volunteer in a homeless shelter in my free time" kind. Universalism breeds obsession and even violence over who is right, rather than encouraging, rewarding, or canonizing the work of scrutiny.

Postmodernism doesn't really offer a replacement for universalism, though. Combined with societal norms, this is why I think individualized reality has taken prominence over a collective one. We deconstructed as if deconstruction was the ultimate goal. This could quite possibly be due to the idea our *direction* has been co-opted by those with power. Their covert redirection of each of us as individuals through promises of empowerment through choice (which they carefully curate) yields many fragile, fragmented perspectives (read: realities) that all operate in service of consumption and capital.

Which prompts the most postmodern question of all time: what is reality?

There are wealthy, prominent figures in one of the United States' biggest industries, technology, who believe the answer is that we live in a computer simulation. And who knows? They *could* be right. Simulation theory posits that reality is running on one or more computers. This requires many assumptions; there must be computers, and they must be powerful enough to run all the physical simulations and render an image for every single person who is connected to or created by the simulation. If each one of our consciousnesses are *generated by the simulation*, then we would all be smaller-scale simulations ourselves, as well. We all make complex observations and choices on a non-stop basis. Are we hardware? Are we software emulation? Are we interfacing with the simulation or are we part of it? These are all questions that must be answered in order to map out even the simplest version of this theory that could be considered "complete."

However, there are significantly less assumptions in believing in a religion. Believing in a religion does not require one to observe all the tenets of it; a great many religious people in the United States subscribe to a very individualized version of the religion they follow. They pick and choose what is "best for them" and ultimately the only collective assumption one is truly required to make as "a believer" is that somehow, someone created all of this. Ultimately, the non-*evidence-derived* assumption you must make is that there's a god (or multiple). See, the holy texts are all human-made.

Among competing hypotheses, the one with the fewest assumptions is often favored as "more likely true," and that the simplest answer is often the correct one. There aren't testable, scientific hypotheses for either of these viewpoints, but simply by number of assumptions, religion is more likely to be true than simulation theory, because religion only requires one: faith.

More important to acknowledge, though, is that neither of these ideas are scientifically testable. I'll go a bit further; I outright believe both simulation theory and religion are incorrect assumptions. *My* viewpoint requires *no* assumptions; *anything* could have happened to bring earth and life around, including, though highly unlikely, the things I believe to be impossibilities. Thing is, really shouldn't matter to one's spiritual beliefs if someone else's don't align fully. The nature of *assumptions* one makes about the nature of the universe needs to be acknowledged as what you perceive to be true without evidence.

This is to say that I am simply stating *my perspective* on these ideas. We have no reason to try to escape perspective because we can't. Similarly, to acknowledge that you're reading my perspective is utterly necessary for the things I say to be valid. If I assert what I believe as fact, I'm essentially saying "everyone is wrong but me." While that *could* be the case, an important thing to remember is that I've arrived at all these conclusions in the same way all human beings do: through observation and reflection.

The "battle for reality" is this: lots of people with differing perspectives want their perspective to be the only one. They believe in objective truth, that a person can act entirely objectively, and that perception can be ignored in the service of universal fact. They also, therefore, have the final answer. I think this is absurd. If we acknowledge that humanity is imperfect, which I do, we must understand that agenda is possible on every level of thought. On top of that, simple imperfection *without* agenda influences how we perceive things.

I want to stress that deconstructive methods are not harmful; finding the very core of something by stripping away all the layers of context, creation, subversion, and anything else people add to concepts, can be good or bad. My concepts are built entirely on top of deconstructive analysis of social and economic norms in the United States.

The phrase "everyone's a critic" is often used to be derisive of other people's opinions. The idea that everyone has something to say that may contradict our perception of personal righteousness prompts a certain defensiveness, too. But if one looks closer, one may see it as an acknowledgement of the basic humanity postmodern philosophy draws from. Everyone *should be*, at the very least internally, analyzing things life brings to their doorstep. Comment or complaint about how things are is often one of the most important steps to take in making a better world. However, many people assume postmodernism is "deconstruction-as-an-ideal."

South Park, for all the criticism I have for it, is an entertaining show and through the years has made some incredibly good observations. It's got its own share of problems, though, ranging from ignorant takes on marginalized people to what I'm getting at in this chapter: the idea that everyone's wrong except you.

Matt Stone and Trey Parker have made it a virtue to find what's wrong with "both sides" and then just call it a day. Stating something is true or false in any capacity means you've "taken a side," and, therefore, you are wrong. The only way to be truly "correct" is to stand above all people, pointing down at them saying, "You fools." Correct is a place in the hierarchy, not a reflection of soundness of statement.

Their show is, in many ways, good, and sometimes even very useful. However, it's also a perfect demonstration of the issue I am attempting to articulate here: if no one is right, then nothing is real. The show doesn't reject meaning; it rejects the pursuit of meaning. Through the years, it seems to have put forward the idea that simply taking everything down will create a situation in which meaning will simply emerge. For a long time, the ending would be when one of the moderate children would deliver a monologue about how we can all be better if we all just stop being so extreme. To put plainly, the work of South Park is taking everything down, not building towards something.

The problem with this is how much it sets the stage for everyone to think their own beliefs are the "non-extreme" ones. If the ideal is the center, then it's best to attempt to paint yourself as the center, even if you aren't. It doesn't really matter whether it's to persuade others or to feel comfortable in the idea you are correct. Being "rational" has become "knowing how all others are wrong."

South Park probably didn't cause society to adopt this viewpoint; it's more likely an avatar for a prevailing belief. Yes, some people probably did grow up on South Park and view reality through this lens. However, I feel this viewpoint was an inevitability with the environment we have been presented. There is no sincerity in shows like "The Bachelor" or "Keeping Up With The Kardashians," nor is there in a news story written to aid a prevailing narrative.

My wife, Ashleigh, and I do a weekly show called "Adversaries," where we deconstruct advertising. We take a commercial and attempt to strip away all the aesthetic and rhetoric to distil the advertisement into something easier to understand and, therefore, easier to find the agenda. When we started it, the goal was to push marketers to stop making advertising that dilutes people, manipulating them and presenting a controlled reality where their product seems to make *everything* much better.

For a *very* short while, we put forward ways in which advertising could do things better. We don't really do that anymore. Through our criticism, we've concluded that the very concept of advertising is built on the manipulation of reality itself and therefore shouldn't be reconstructed. The most bizarre thing about this is that advertising itself is little more than an acknowledgement of the intended customers' biases framed through aspiration.

Advertising demands an individualist view. For it to succeed on the level its architects wish it to, a person must not be looking beyond their own moral and intellectual authority. You have just been presented with new information, and you must decide based on it. If you look beyond the new information, you begin to tap into the collective understanding. However, if you accept its attempts to tie your feelings and identity to products, services, and lifestyles, you're customizing your own reality using a toolkit provided by capital. You're painting a picture with a palette handed to you by Sprite. It's not a trick; it's you making a decision based on choices within the curated environment that's presented to you. You are not under control; the toolkit, the palette, or the environment is.

We regularly get asked why we treat advertising so seriously. In today's America, all things are advertising. Every presentation of ideology, representation of events, all hot takes, *everything is advertising*. South Park tried to present this concept during a season that is a lot better in its base assumptions than in its presentation. They ran a multi-episode plot arc in which advertisements were sentient beings wishing to take over society. Their anthropomorphizing of advertising is actually brilliant, and represented what could have been a large progression in their approach. However, that season also attacked "politically correct culture," even if only at face value to make a larger point. I'm probably a bit more lenient about that specific plot arc than a lot of public leftists. I think "PC Culture" was possibly intended as a stand-in for neoliberalism, or perhaps they are inches away from understanding that the gentrification of language is related to neoliberalism's marketization of everything. The likelihood that a regular South Park viewer, a comedy fan rather than an economic theory buff, would take this away from their viewing is extremely low, though. The season ended up being a bit disjointed, with a lot of concepts that were presented through an unempathetic, angry narrative that was designed to maintain their "both sides" cred. So close and yet so far.

Everything that gets presented in media is meant to persuade you in some way. It maybe to get you to laugh *or* it may be to get you to believe that men are somehow in a worse position than women societally. What is strange, however, is that we automatically accept advertising as a convention of American life. The construct of advertising pays for all the things we like to watch so it can't be *that* bad. Mr. Robot, a show about distrust in the systems around us, wouldn't exist if it weren't for advertising. Which advertising, of course, asks you to place your trust in that very system. Because of this, it can only tangentially mention certain things. It can't give you specifics and it must come off as *maybe* only possible in fiction.

If the show worked tirelessly to persuade you to opt-out of modern American life, no company would run ads on it. If no one wanted to run ads on it, it wouldn't have a home on the USA Network. This is controlled opposition; the show itself is very good, but ultimately something in it (or excluded from it) must encourage you to prefer the comfort of the status quo, or just not encourage you to resist it. Given what the show is, it still must feel as though you're somehow resisting by engaging in this *rebellious* act of... watching a TV show that's supported by advertising.

Whether or not this is intentional, I can't tell you. I'm sure for some marketers and content creators, it is. For others, it may just be some version of "we can't depict violence as good," without understanding that there is a difference between retaliatory violence against the system and violence against individuals or marginalized groups. For others, it's a fight in a boardroom about censorship of art.

Without deconstruction, our analysis of these things will never be complete, partly, because we need to look at all aspects of something at their base levels and, partly, because advertising itself has been deconstructed by people who want to build a more effective framework on top of the things that they deem already valuable. The building part is not postmodernism; it's drawn from whatever philosophical approach those with agenda favor. The point is, they had to start somewhere.

Deconstruction of societal norms to examine their worth *is good*, there's just always going to be difference in intent. Some may wish to deconstruct to attain more understanding and, therefore, a better grasp on the world, while others may do it with naked exploitation in mind.

When we expose the reasons that we hold things to be true, we may find that we are propping up ideas that are harmful or just plain wrong. However, if deconstruction is the only ideal from the philosophy we engage in, then we will always end up with little more than debris. In the case of specific societal norms that end up being harmful, that may well be a good thing.

In the case of *everything*, however... not so much.

PETER COFFIN

3. DENIAL OF A COLLECTIVE REALITY

If there was an alternate world in which you were all-powerful, where everything bent to your will, including reality itself, would you want to live there? What would you give up to take residence?

What if, technically speaking, it wasn't real? *To you*, it's real, but to no one else. Is the "real" world, the one inhabited by others, real? Also, what is real?

To quote the Matrix (because, come on; *you knew I would eventually*), "if real is what you can feel, smell, taste and see, then 'real' is simply electrical signals interpreted by your brain." So, what if the world everyone else is living in is fake? What if the imaginary world we just made up, but also the "real" world, are fake?

Let's say you can prove the imaginary world is fake, but you can't prove the "real" world *is real*. You wield power in the imaginary world, while in the "real" world, you and those around you have none.

Would you rather live in something specifically constructed for you, as an individual, or would you rather live in a world where our experience is shared? Philosopher Robert Nozick poised similar questions in his 1974 book *Anarchy, State, and Utopia*. His main purpose was to refute hedonism, the idea that all good is derived from pleasure. Though I don't necessarily believe pleasure is the only thing good is derived from, I am not asking this question to debunk anything. I'm asking because it seems like many have made the choice unconsciously.

Love has the capability to make life both horrible and wonderful. However, does that power exist if the party giving you love doesn't have the ability to choose? Further, do you define the criteria from which they choose? Is that love? Does that feel the same?

Can love be simulated? Fully?

I don't think so; reciprocal love necessitates participation from all parties, and knowing it's one-sided creates a sour smell. The smell is not unlike a refrigerator containing fresh produce but also a carton of sour milk that's been left open. It is the smell of a poopy diaper in a trash can where someone forgot to close the lid; you only smell it a little, but you smell it *everywhere in the house*.

If you don't have the ability to create what we call "true love" in your simulation, are you *actually* all powerful? What if you don't need love? What if you are beyond love? What if this *isn't* something that matters to you? What if you totally ignore the human meaning that we've ascribed to love and view it simply as a chemical reaction? What if you are unable or unwilling to acknowledge that, for many people, the sum may be more than the parts?

This isn't a success or a failure; it is "the individual" in practice. The lack of need for something that's impossible to reproduce virtually might make a self-contained virtual life work out pretty well *for that individual*. That said, in retreating to such a life, one also may be prioritizing oneself above every other human being. Individuals all have different situations and motives, though.

To some of this mind, one's ability to live in a perfect world matters more than what they can do to improve an imperfect one. To them, it's an elitism and a greed entirely familiar to our current world and, sadly, shouldn't sound that absurd. To escape into a perfectly tailored virtual life and leave the rest of the world to fend for themselves, one would have to be, well, selfish.

To that effect, I think Ayn Rand would *really* like virtual reality. Her ideology of "rational self-interest" melds incredibly well with a loveless ultimate power simulator.

Rationally speaking, love is absurd. No one acting only in their own rational self-interest would engage in it; love causes one's priorities to center less on oneself. Love breeds attachment and fondness. The result of "true love" is some degree of selflessness. Not necessarily to the degree of a Tibetan Monk, mind you.

Love, however, is inherently collective. At least, it is if you look at it as a human feeling rather than a "strategy for mate selection." Love can be romantic, platonic, familial, or societal, and these are all collective adjectives. Love for, and I must emphasize *only for*, oneself is selfishness at best.

That said, I do hope you love yourself and who you are. You have absolutely no reason not to; you are a biological wonder on the basest level and yet you are so much more. You have a personality, a moral compass, wants, needs, and everything that comes with being among the most complex life on this planet. Though the water flea has about 25% more genes than you and me, but you don't need to spend several hours googling that.

Depending on how close to my description you personally feel, it's probably not just yourself that you love. I'd bet you love someone out there for genuine reasons. You may not feel it at the same level all the time. That feeling may be in the past, associated with a deceased person, animal or something else. It's not necessarily romantic, platonic, familial, or even something I want to rigidly define for you. You know it when you feel it. It is there.

Otherwise, *why wouldn't you just abandon this place to live in a world where you were all-powerful?* Why would you care if it's not "real?" If you had no attachment to this world, why bother? Fully individualized custom realities exist in many forms, some noticeable and overt while others might be totally imperceptible to even ourselves. But in absolutely none of them does there exist a feeling of genuine love, and that is why I think you're still participating in our admittedly struggling collective reality.

I've played video games since I was five years old. We got a Nintendo Entertainment System in 1989 and I have loved them ever since. There's something amazing about being able to experience a different place or something that's totally impossible and video games most certainly allow you to do that.

Gaming isn't just a platform for creativity and entertainment, though. It's a *place*; one where you can feel like you're "more" or "bigger." That's not to say in the physical world, you definitely feel "small." It's just that most of us don't have any significant power to fight injustice or even just demand a raise at a job we don't love. In gaming, though, one accumulates points, trophies, achievements, and gets to be The Chosen One™ in a million different scenarios. In the physical world, one must compete with 7.5 billion other people. Video games let you insert a disc or download a few gigs of data and *POOF! You're a special boy!*

That's not an assertion that video games are little more than simply flattery to the player. Complex, thoughtful tales and amazing gameplay experiences exist in abundance. There just happens to also be a significant number of video games that can be boiled down to simply a power fantasy. It's very profitable to sell people a means to feel powerful when the world they would occupy otherwise alienates them, rendering them disenfranchised and powerless, is easier than selling them a reminder that the power dynamics of the world do not favor a person in their position.

The power fantasy of these types of video games is that you, too, can be a hero, a genius, and a Casanova simply by fulfilling mission criteria. Gaming can present us with simplified versions of complex human issues, from violence, to mystery, to relationships, and I think that's where a serious problem begins to set in: in the physical world, these things are not missions. We do not have objectives that can be completed or conditions to be met which guarantee success. There are no checkpoints or cheats.

Violence has complex motivations and ramifications that can't simply be solved by rationalizing. Crimes go for decades without being solved. A relationship based on the idea that if you do A, B, and C, then you will get a Blowjob Bonus is not something anyone should ever simply expect. I'm not saying it's impossible, but it's incredibly unlikely. People aren't games.

What are video games? Ultimately, they're just computer programs. They're loops of instructions essentially dictating logic; "if this, then that." It is important to highlight that this is not even vaguely like how human logic works. For better or worse, we are much more complicated. We can have multiple motives, multiple desired outcomes, contingency plans, we work on assumptions and then have to shift gears. We fuck up in both small and extraordinary ways. We contradict ourselves regularly. We can absorb numerous layers of meaning from almost anything: the personal, metaphysical, contextual, or existential. We don't take everything literally and we don't always mean the same things even if we repeat ourselves.

The way things really are in our world is wholly dissimilar to the mode of operation many video games prime players to exercise. Cause and effect is certainly real but if we view life through a rigid lens of "if I do this thing, this other thing I want will happen!" This breeds a sense of entitlement. "If I'm nice to a woman, I'll get sex" is one of the most time-honored misconceptions this kind of thinking can result in. That said, I'm not asserting that video games make a person think simply being nice gets you laid, because they do not. Still, after ongoing conditioning in this way, one might experience disappointment at the world for not holding up its end of the bargain.

Through repeated consumption of a curated, abridged version of an experience, it may be that people can be led to believe that if one fulfills a certain specification, they will be rewarded in kind. This "win conditioning" could help to form identity, acting as both carrot and stick, the establishment of rewards and consequences directing who a person is.

Winning would be looked at as a celebratory event and a loss as questioning of one's validity as a person. Losing is then not a learning experience, *it's proof of the deficiency of who loses* and one cannot allow oneself to be viewed that way in a society of supposed merit. If we view social interaction through this lens, we will always be seeking a payoff. We're trying to "win," and additionally, we want the "good ending."

The more profit-driven aspects of this serve to consume and gamify social interaction and it yields an expectation or "product" that one is investing their time and attention into. I believe this results in an injured way of seeing the world, as well as seemingly unrelated to the stated purpose of any artistic medium. Most of these results come from the business end of the project's necessity to profit. Often, art must acquiesce to the need to be a satisfying purchase, either one time without refund or repeatedly in smaller transactions.

Video games have been quickly adopted into the societal canon as an incredibly effective platform for both artists and businesses. Like radio, television, books, and all the many works of fiction created in these mediums, video games allow a mind to run wild in situations one will likely never physically experience, and they can tell us something about our own lives. They stimulate us and make us think.

They're capable of being both very powerful and very empowering.

For those with disabilities they can be more than empowering. In fact, and as we develop virtual reality, society may be able to further empower them. While advances do slowly bring more of this to fruition, we often look to the future in science fiction.

The series-defining episode of the popular Netflix series *Black Mirror*, "San Junipero," is one of those serendipitous cross-sections of several types of media that somehow does significantly more than any one of the mediums it exists in or critiques. On the surface, it's the love story of two people in a strange place. As it progresses, we realize the characters are dealing with serious issues: severe disability and terminal illness. Ultimately, because of the virtual world they're given the opportunity to inhabit, they fall in love and begin a life together that will last as long as they wish. This riveting sci-fi depiction of a love impossible in the physical world portrays a very specific context, though, and either quietly or accidentally addresses something very important about virtual reality.

When life is over and our bodies die, would it be *bad* to live in a perfect world, even if not entirely real? No; I think that'd be pretty damn good. Few would turn it down; it's essentially Heaven. A lot of us have given up on such a thing.

Similarly, when someone is paralyzed, injured, ill, marginalized, or otherwise affected beyond their control and to their own detriment, is an alternate reality somehow bad? Someone wishing to occupy a world in which they are no longer limited by their situation in the physical world deserves very little criticism. Limitations and discrimination could be sidestepped, leaving them with a *possibly* more emotionally fulfilling experience. Similarly, a person starving to death due to extreme poverty would likely prefer a virtual world where they can craft pizza into existence (or just never feel hunger) over one where they live in destitution. I wouldn't call these scenarios bad or unproductive, in no small part because I try not to be an ass.

However, let's flip the whole thing. Imagine that San Junipero was a story between two young, healthy, completely able, straight, *wealthy* people with the ways and means to live exactly the way they want. Doesn't it feel just a bit wrong?

Those people get to live in *our* world however they wish to. They get whatever they want, on demand, and hold real power. Their existence travels along a path they get to define for themselves, and they experience the real world in a manner that makes a controllable, virtual one superfluous. Yet, these are the people who can get their hands on virtual reality; it's always been expensive, and it's being engineered to profit. It makes perfect business sense as a luxury product; those who hoard power because they want power will *obviously* buy a thing that lets them experience ultimate power.

We often talk about the privilege of being straight, white, or male. But we discuss the able-bodied, healthy and neurotypical a lot less in that context. We don't often talk about physical health as a privilege, much less mental health; Americans live in a country with a for-profit health system that exacerbates many curable issues, and the cure always boils down to money. It's important to recognize that it's not always quantifiable how anyone deemed something other than "normal" is punished in our society. Not to mention the fact that the aspirational programming and lifestyle content of our media rarely focuses on the impoverished. It's much harder to get people to go buy stuff *if they have no money.*

There are many ways in which this world can be totally unbearable. The beauty in "San Junipero" was the enabling of two people, one entirely unable to physically move, and another with failing health. These two were given a place where they could be able and healthy. They could live lives that the "real" world didn't afford them the opportunity to experience—and with those limitations gone from their lives, they fell in love. The profound sublimity and raw potential of the ideas on display was nothing short of beautiful.

Now, for a moment, again consider synthetic reality and artificial intelligence in the context of Palmer Luckey and all the other straight, white, cis, able-bodied, healthy, wealthy young men working to make it happen. Do they actually *need* an alternate world where an age-old patriarchal fantasy where consent is not an issue, where sex is an executable program, comes true—where all things are possible and dependent only on desire? Where money is no object and reality itself is subject to their whims?

No, but they *want* one.

To be clear, it's certainly alright to want your own personal space. Still, I believe the current push for VR is more about finding the lamp and getting your wishes, than about that. To have unlimited power in your own personal space rather than just to have it seems to be the real focus.

So... Ready Player One, a book and upcoming film. It's exactly that.

VR is headed for a place of wish fulfillment, ignorance, and insensitivity to people experiencing real problems. Hell, the protagonist of Ready Player One is living a destitute existence in a corporate dystopia in which they escape to a virtual world called The Oasis and the book can't even be bothered to give a shit about *that*. "We must save the Oasis..." As if the Oasis isn't clearly a platitude offered in exchange for inaction regarding the hopeless decay of society. The neurotypical, fully abled, cis, white male protagonist chooses the Oasis over working on making the world better for everyone. There's a shock.

"But... But it's about stopping an evil corporation from monetizing the Oasis!" To that I say, "so what?" The plot isn't about *ending* the Oasis or fighting back against the conditions people are forced to live in, *so I believe it's the wrong plot for the world described in the book.* Ready Player One, published over a decade after The Matrix was released, is a book set very obviously in a dystopia where people connect to a virtual world because their material conditions are so terrible. The Oasis is defined quite explicitly as escapism rather than liberation, and the story is not about making its inhabitants' lives better. Instead, it's about the protagonist becoming the rich owner of virtual property.

But can we really expect much more from a book where there is an ongoing energy crisis, but most people spend the majority of their time in a shared, photo-realistic simulation in which anything is possible? Forget Bitcoin, Oasis would be a hell of a power suck.

The ultimate point of Ready Player One is a race to find a MacGuffin that makes you GOD KING OF ESCAPISM WORLD. It is in no way concerned with power structure or oppression. It doesn't want to talk about what the Oasis could be in terms of a tool for helping people, instead it is a distraction and this is a good thing. The plot genuinely is "white man turns on his VR and gets everything he could dream of, including material wealth and a romantic relationship."

I'd call that a far cry from the beautiful situation in which two marginalized people were able to experience what would be completely impossible otherwise. If today's VR companies succeed on the trajectory they are on, it seems likely that situations like San Junipero will be no more than a byproduct, if anything at all, while Oases will spring up constantly for people to race Deloreans with Ghostbusters logos on the side, wearing custom outfits they got out of a loot box.

Or worse... the USS Callister, another episode of *Black Mirror* in which artificial intelligence copies of people are kept in a simulation to serve as punching bags for a man who wishes he had more control over their real-life counterparts.

It's with a certain reverence we should criticize indulgence of video games or VR. For some, these changing mediums that give hope and form community. But for others, I'll quote from a brilliant song by Gorillaz: "don't get lost in Heaven, they got locks on the gates."

This line means a great deal to me, personally. The eponymous song "Don't Get Lost In Heaven" is seemingly about cocaine addiction, though I take it more generally speaking; "getting lost in Heaven" means having too much of a thing you deem to be good. "They got locks on the gates" means if you've gone too far, you can't come back. They've got you for good.

Demon Days, the album this song is on, is about the ruin of the Earth at the hands of humanity. It's a quintessential album of its time, discussing the war in Iraq and other destruction we've wrought as a species—in ecological terms as much as personal ones. It's an album that totally fucks me up every time I listen to it, and it might be my favorite one of all time. I say all this because I want you to understand just how important this specific line is to understand how I read the denial of a collective reality: we are all, individually, lost in our own personal Heaven.

So what's the good thing we're getting too much of? Ourselves.

Individualism is a social outlook that emphasizes the importance of the individual at the moral level—that it is moral for the individual to be the most important thing, also making the individual the highest moral authority. One's goals and desires are not just one's drive, but also one's *value*. The hyper-individualism of the United States of America considers independence and self-reliance to be godlike. The individual is believed to hold precedence over any group.

The customer is always right.

Before I continue, I want to note that the idea of individuality is good. The notion that we are all individuals with unique skills, thoughts, feelings, etc. *is healthy*. Contrary to how media has painted the collectivist viewpoint through the years, acting as a hive mind is a physical impossibility for humans, and if we were asked to operate as one, life would suck. We neither need or deserve that. We are all different people with complicated sets of circumstances that there is no singular method to put oneself into a better situation, and it's important to acknowledge this. Life is obviously not one-size-fits-all.

But none of us are the only person on the planet, either.

That's where The Religion of Me, individualism, comes in as a core societal philosophy. When the individual holds precedence over all other things, the individual's choice can only be at the center of all things.

Imagine more and more people believing that VR is better than real life.

So, then, what is virtual reality? Is it specifically a medium in which to create and/or experience things, or could it be the most elaborate "alternative fact" of all? Does it even matter if this is a computer simulation when your outlook is based purely on belief? Do you believe that Sandy Hook was a hoax put on by actors? That there was no Holocaust? Did we land on the moon?

Do you need the objects around you to be simulated by a computer to live in that world?

This is the cross-section of individualism and win conditioning: if I lose, but simply believe I didn't, *then I didn't lose*. In fact, I win. Very black-and-white thinking combines with an individualist view on reality and one's own relationship with it. One may find the necessity to create a custom version of the world one lives in that doesn't violate one's identity.

I don't believe in telling people the internet isn't real life because I met my wife on it. We've been married since 2012 and if you'd have told me our long-distance, online relationship was fake, I'd have told you to fuck off. The internet is all of the following at once: a video game, virtual

44

reality, real life, attachment and detachment. Its oscillation between contradictory ideas is fascinating. It's amazing something can be so many things that are seemingly mutually exclusive.

My wife and I loved each other before we physically met and that was not a simulation. The internet itself is not a fantasy world by default; it's a tool—one that can be used to create a fantasy world. It's not just a tool for you and me, though. It is as much a medium for governments and corporate entities to do as they wish in, as well.

The way the world currently works often puts governments *in service of corporate entities* so let's focus on the corporate agenda: profit.

So how does one profit on the internet? Well, let's talk about how Google does it. When you go to google.com and type in a thing, Google learns from it. The more things you tell it that you want to hear, the more it knows what you want to hear. The best thing Google can do is give you what you want—because that makes Google useful for you.

What if you want information that is provably false? *Does Google benefit from telling you it's false?* If Google repeatedly tells you that you're seeking false information (read: that what you want confirmed or debunked cannot be) are you as likely to keep using Google? Don't answer "yes" on principle, either. You've searched for validation on Google. We all have. We've all gotten it, too.

Google's most profitable feedback loops include something like this: user searches for "climate change," then gets the answer they already believe, and the site that gives it to them displays Google ads. Or, even better, the site that gives them that information buys the ad space directly above the search results. You know, the ad space that *really* looks like search results?

"A Declaration of the Independence of Cyberspace" by John Perry Barlow is widely considered to be one of the most important things ever written about the internet. If you haven't read it, it's pretty much a rebuke of the physical world's power over that of the budding civilization of the internet. Indeed, it's essentially a rebuke of power itself; it mentions protecting individuals' opinions "no matter how singular," and the concept of "enlightened self-interest."

Some consider it to be anarchist, but I think that had Ayn Rand had not been dead for 14 years when Barlow published it, she'd likely have gotten behind it. Anarchy understands and recognizes power and believes in working to distribute it, so it cannot create unjust hierarchy, while Barlow simply rebukes the idea altogether.

> *Cyberspace consists of transactions, relationships, and thought itself, arrayed like a standing wave in the web of our communications. Ours is a world that is both everywhere and nowhere, but it is not where bodies live. We are creating a world that all may enter without privilege or prejudice accorded by race, economic power, military force, or station of birth. We are creating a world where anyone, anywhere may express his or her beliefs, no matter how singular, without fear of being coerced into silence or conformity.*

This sounds great, but the underlying ethos does not account for the distribution of power. Instead of talking in any way about power structure, it views liberty as a sort of "god mode," as one might say in the parlance of video games.

When the concept of the individual becomes society's most important thing, society doesn't function, because *society is collective.* "Fact" is collective.

The acceptance of evidence is the basis of collective reality. Without agreeing we all see that rock that looks *kinda like a scrotum,* we don't know that everyone saw it. If someone didn't see it, they can't remember it. If postmodern deconstruction exposes and criticizes just how fragile the collective concept of fact is, individualism is the ideology that takes advantage of that fragility.

It's as tempting to dictate one's own reality as it is terrifying to find out to what extent one is already doing it. You know who and what you believe. You know who talks like you talk and what makes you feel at ease. That's what's right for you and you can never be wrong about that, right?

But what happens when everyone is off in their own perfect-for-them world? What happens when no one cares about what happens to other people because those people tried to tell me I'm wrong? What happens when "the people" act more like "a lot of persons?"

My thought is this would become a power vacuum. While we're occupying a fantasy where we all weigh 20 pounds less, people who want it all *are taking it.* These people don't care what we think and feel; they just want money and power. When they move, we're preoccupied and don't see it.

There are more than a few reasons someone might want to curate an environment encouraging this denial.

Scrutiny starts as the act of an individual thinking critically and then spreads as more people with similar observations repeat these criticisms to each other. If people get to talking about something that's *just a bit off*, their words will likely find new ears, possibly infecting them with aversion to the thing in question. Wouldn't it make sense to address it where it starts; to vaccinate, rather than treat an epidemic? If you can head scrutiny off at the pass, why not do it?

Companies, governments, and other people who wish to consolidate power specifically for themselves can either rule through force or manipulation of environment. If everyone is encouraged to believe that the buck stops with them, if we're all the protagonist of our own movie, if we're placed at the center of our own little universe where *it really seems like everything revolves around us*, then we're encouraged to be critical of each other *more than those with power*.

It's not as if none of us deserve criticism, but if the criticism one brings is "the world doesn't revolve around *you*," then it might be useful to ask oneself "does my world also revolve around myself?"

You're required to be a leader in a squad of one because everyone in the world is doing the exact same thing. You must defer to you, otherwise what do you even have in this world? And when everyone's competing with everyone over whose facts are real and whose are "alternative," those who understand why and how this is going on can *take everything they want*.

The denial of collective reality is the ultimate tool to those who want more and more power. It's accomplished by presenting every single individual with a world that customizes itself to their individual preference and tells them that everyone who doesn't agree is wrong. It has no allegiance to narrative—for every Fox News, there's an MSNBC; for every Breitbart, there's a ShareBlue. Also, Verrit happened and it is *hilarious*. These are all the result of indulging narrative that reinforces one's own perspective.

Custom reality is there *for you*. It's the default. You don't opt-in to it any more than you would opt-in to what country you're born. It mirrors you, so any scrutiny towards it is scrutiny towards *you*. It's uncomfortable to say, "I'm wrong," and for good reason: it's legitimately good to believe in yourself.

But you can't treat yourself like your own personal savior, either...

PETER COFFIN

4. THE RELIGION OF ME

Six thousand years ago, God created the Heavens and the Earth. Right?

I mean, that seems real to me. Nothing seems inherently strange about that statement. My neighbor and my family think so too. So, it's real, right? I mean, I have never looked in to carbon dating and everyone I've ever spoken to thinks it's just a test from God to see if we all *really* believe. My friends and family would never lie to me, so I believe in what they believe in.

I'm hoping what I've done here can illustrate a couple of things.

First: collective reality, the thing I'm advocating for in this book, is not automatically scientific or evidence-based.

Second: collective reality, the thing I'm advocating for in this book, is also not automatically *correct*. There's a very specific danger in the idea that we all must work toward agreement on what reality is: that we're wrong.

Religion *is a collective reality* in the way I'm using the term. This prompts the question: why hasn't that been enough? This book has repeatedly said that a collective reality is what we should strive for and will continue to do so. But why have previous collective realities not held the world together in the way I hope one eventually could?

Most obviously, there's more than one religion. Less obviously, religions constantly evolve. People believe in different things and every single one of those things has changed in some way over the many years we humans have been using our rods and cones to take in light waves, and assigning meaning through interpreting the spectrum of radiation to which we've grown sensitive. Religion evolves with society and the biggest piece of evidence I'd submit in support is the Old Testament.

The Old Testament pretty much tells us to stone everything that isn't a nuclear family, though we didn't start using that term at a societal level until the 1950s. If they're not behaving in a manner that creates more human beings while following the established hierarchy, you stone 'em.

Gay guys? Stone 'em. Ladies showing their ankles? Stone 'em. Slaves doing something that isn't labor? Stone 'em. Pile of stones? Stone... wait, I can't stone these stones with... these stones! I have failed! I'm sorry for my transgressions, oh Lord! Please have mercy, Lord! Hallowed be thy name! Hosanna! Amen!

Man acting overly apologetic to avoid a stoning for being unable to stone *stones* with themselves? Stone 'em.

Ever notice how we *don't* stone people for doing stuff the Old Testament says we *can* stone them for? Christians don't even seem to get Stone Thirsty™ when you break the commandments; in fact, many of them don't even care. These folks simply believe in God and Jesus; they believe there is good in the world and that these entities are the reason why. Many call the Bible, both the Old and New Testaments, a metaphorical book, one not meant to be taken literally. Still others outright ignore the book itself, creating churches that welcome people who view others from the same gender in a romantic light, which is explicitly banned in the Bible. Perhaps they even go so far as to properly recognize and accommodate people who don't conform to a binary, which would probably really freak Paul or Matthew right out. I doubt The Disciples™ had even thought of gender-as-a-spectrum or any alternative to a binary of genders.

Religion isn't the same thing it was a century ago. In the United States, we've gone from Puritan slave owners to drug-taking, anti-racist, anti-war hippies, and then to unknowing servants of godless, capitalist rulers who are always looking for new ways to separate the people, to isolate us, prevent us from feeling whole. Endless consumption is the endgame, telling us we may one day find something that fills the empty hole in our hearts left by our inability to form a fulfilling identity in a space crowded with logos and slogans all meant to manipulate who we are.

The genuinely religious among us are, thankfully, less dogmatic than they once were. I don't understand why people criticize Christians for "picking and choosing." When I see someone do it, I can't help but think to myself that it's a good thing the stoning stopped at some point. Does that person really just want to be able to do rock murders?

That individuals *preserve the good things* about religion, dropping more and more of the bad, is not only positive, but some degree of evidence that humanity is good at its core. It is right to purge the kind of stuff that only leads to unending aggression. Any philosophy preaching hatred doesn't deserve acceptance in my book.

And this is my book.

Religion is seen by some as universal truth, but as I said earlier, it is collective truth. In this book, I'll endlessly prattle on about my bullshit. You will hear many variations on the notion that collective reality is the antidote to custom reality, but it's also important to keep in mind that even life-saving medicine is imperfect.

The price of a collective reality with holes in it, from inconsistencies to moral lapses, is that individuals may opt-out. Whether that means saying "I don't take the Old Testament literally" or totally not believing in God *is all up to the individual.* Individuality, in this context, is incredibly important. It is imperative that we can form opinions that contradict established ideas if they seem questionable, and equally so that we attempt to corroborate what we are saying.

If a collective reality is based around traditions and norms that people eventually question, it stands to reason that individuals will break off from that. They do not trust the reality presented to them anymore and must begin the process of adjusting their perspective to feel as though things again make sense. I perceive this as reality individualizing; as an individual finds answers for themselves they become the curator of their custom reality.

"Good" collective reality must be based on standardized acceptance of evidence. If not, it wouldn't really be a good faith attempt at a conclusion. That would make our agreement on what is real, nothing more than *argumentum ad populum*, or, a fallacious argument to popularity. Popular consensus involves relying on the opinions of a lot of people who do not necessarily have all the information, so I think it would be better to collectivize through scientific methodology, material dialectics, or some other evidence-based method of discussing and testing the material validity of a claim or observation.

Collective reality can be good or bad, but we must acknowledge that *it is also custom reality.* All reality is.

If a collective reality is *not* rooted in evidence and our understanding of it, the likelihood of it falling apart under scrutiny grows. That people can interpret evidence in different ways further complicates the issue. More people fragment off and create their own individual variants, finding what they are comfortable believing and forgetting everything else.

This has become a standardized mode of operation; what is "best for you" according to a news feed or search engine may lead you in a totally different direction than those around you. People are meant to emerge as the leader of their own little world. As the collective reality of specific dogma (religious or otherwise) dissipates, we are encouraged to centralize *ourselves* in our belief structure. We become our own savior. The customer is always right.

I've heard people say, "everyone thinks they're the protagonist of their own movie" to try to shame folks for thinking they're special. I don't think this is productive; I do think everyone is special and I'm not afraid to say cornball shit like that. I just don't think everyone should get to prioritize their own reality running as a perpetual validation machine. There really is no "objective truth" if you are a being of perspective, and humans are. This seems ever more apparent as people reject the dogma of religion, or indeed religion itself, with their own versions of these age-old beliefs.

Our religion is *us* as individuals. We're our own personal Jesus. Lift up the receiver, I'll make you a believer.

"Believe in yourself," everyone says on repeat in every corner of our lives. Certainly, love and belief in oneself are important components to a fulfilling identity, but how much farther are we all asked to go? Well, how much growth is enough for a publicly traded company on the stock market? Is the answer "infinite?" Why yes! Not only is that how business works, but it's how you're supposed to do everything, too!

"Believe in yourself," your teacher tells you as they hope you score well in standardized tests, ensuring they keep their jobs another year.

"Believe in yourself," your boss tells you as they decline to give you a raise, but will "revisit your productivity report in a few months."

"Believe in yourself," the corporate trainer tells you when you ask about accountability protocols, hoping you feel good enough about their answer not to put the question to their superiors later.

If any of these things go awry, it's certainly just that you didn't believe enough in yourself, right? You need to believe in yourself more! Believe more, okay? Clap to tell your inner Tinkerbell you believe! Why aren't you clapping? Do you not believe? CLAP, ASSHOLE. LOUDER. THIS ISN'T LOUD ENOUGH.

GREAT JOB. YOU KILLED TINKERBELL.

We don't get the privilege of doubting ourselves or our actions. No, I don't mean insecurity, because we're never meant to stop feeling that. I mean that re-evaluating the course we're on is seen as a weakness. We can't be wrong too often, so the best thing to be is never wrong. The best way not to be wrong in an environment where the individual is the key authority on all things is to simply believe you are right. When you believe you are right, you feel confident in your facts. When you feel confident, you look confident. When you look confident, you're taken to have a reason to be confident. You must be right!

The competitive environment that is modern, American life all but eliminates our ability to be wrong, which then also limits our capacity to learn by the experience of being wrong. "Wrong" must never be acknowledged internally or extremely.

As pressure mounts to be perfect, incentive to have a different definition of "perfect" rises. If "perfect" means "perfect by your own standards," then being perfect is as easy as forming beliefs that don't contradict anything in your life. It's as easy as ignoring any internal or external push for you to develop. If you need to develop, that means you aren't already perfect. And you are! Right?

Taste is something that we should be able to apply to low-stakes situations without major conflict, yet *every* situation involving taste has an element of garbage behavior. This is where we see what I believe to be the conflation of taste and value.

Since taste diverges so much between people, it often becomes a priority to convince people you are the one with *good* taste. Now, there really is no such thing as good taste or bad taste; the actual distinction is just yours and mine. But because we have accepted the position that we must always be correct, we are willing to contort our own perception to remain truthful. We must honestly believe we are correct, which also means *having the best taste*.

This means caring about the review scores of films and video games. "I like movies that have good Rotten Tomatoes scores and I hate ones with bad scores! That means I have good taste! Wait, it looks like people enjoy this film I do not enjoy. I must coordinate on anonymous message boards to fill the user reviews with scores that will bring its average down! Muahahahahahaha!" For video games, replace "Rotten Tomatoes" with "Metacritic."

It's about what you believe and trying to make others think that it's the prevailing belief.

One can truthfully say one is nice if, by one's own standards for "nice," one is nice. Maybe this hypothetical person holds doors for a first date, but when that doesn't make their date fall head over heels, they act standoffish or mean. The person might think they acted nicely and are just reacting to someone being mean to them. But what if their date suspected they might change tone based on a small slight and considers *that* not nice? Is that the date's failing, or is that the "nice" person's?

What if a trans person was denied a bank loan, despite having great credit? The loan agent they were working with to apply for the loan acted perfectly "nicely" about it, but it's the millionth time the trans person has heard the phrase "there's nothing I can do" this year, despite doing everything right. Is that "nice," or is it just cordial? Is it the loan agent? Is it the trans issues? Why won't anyone help the trans person? The loan agent may truly think they are good on trans issues but also just made a trans person's life harder for no reason.

On the other hand, how *mean* is it to draw negative attention to some guy groping women on the subway? It's certainly going to *sound* mean. It would most likely include some harsh language that will insult him and make him feel bad. He's going to go home and feel hurt by the mean person on the subway who yelled at him. Was it truly mean, though?

Uh, no. It was not. The only mean thing that happened is some jackass grabbing folks' body parts without consent. *That is the mean thing here.*

According to *me*, anyhow. I'm sure the imaginary groper thinks he's harmless. Both of us are living in different realities with separate sets of rules, ultimately chosen by the individual. The Divine here, the one dictating what is the acceptable behavior, is us. Seriously, though, fuck that guy I made up.

The strength of religion through the ages is that everything you needed to know was *just right there*. If one followed a religion with an afterlife, one just had to follow those instructions and would end up in a great situation for all eternity after death. Whether this is right or wrong, I don't pretend to know. I don't personally believe in it, but my opinion is not the cause; it's the effect.

When Charles Darwin put forward his theory of evolution, he met a lot of resistance from religious people. In fact, he still does, despite being very dead. There's more personal reasons for why this was a huge problem for the religious on an individual level, but let's talk about what this has done on a macro level.

The more the theory of evolution was tested through the years, the more correct and useful its main assertions proved to be. We have mapped the human genome at this point. We will likely be able to mass clone replacement organs sometime in the future and that wouldn't be possible without starting at Darwin. This was also a significant disruption to not just a belief structure, but a way of life for billions of people. For many, it was the end of an era. All this proving of information that harms one's belief structure *triggered the grieving process en masse*.

Here's something interesting about the grieving process: a lot of people do not get past the first stage of denial. Some do and move to anger, lashing out at scientific research that has repeatable results. Still, the farthest some go is bargaining.

Negotiating with the loss of even just an aspect of one's belief structure is the single most individualist thing a person can do. It's not easy to find an acceptable rationale to allow one to maintain a belief structure after it has been proven flawed on some level, and people do it *just because their identity is threatened.*

This isn't to be critical of people who believe there's no reason to stone a woman to death for having lied about having sex before marriage, as Deuteronomy 22:20-21 implies. I think if you can mentally say, "I believe in God, but I do not believe in this," then you've proven to have had both a moral center and a backbone, even if you've only had to use it in the most internalized of ways. Remember, a holy text authentically says this, but most religious people do *not* think this.

Holiness is the state of being consecrated to God or a religious purpose. One doesn't fuck with holy stuff; it could damn you to hell. It takes a lot of chutzpah to say: "I don't care if going against this book may lead to eternal damnation, I'm not actually going to kill this cheating piece of shit. I just want them to fuck off and get out of my life!"

I commend a person for knowing that is wrong and embracing a kinder version of their faith and simply cursing at people instead of committing nonmetallic mineral homicide. Similarly, I commend the people who totally reject the religion due to its foundation in cruel ideas such as this (though it should be said that patriarchy isn't exclusively a problem of religion). In fact, I commend *anyone* who doesn't stone people for not being virgins, regardless of motive. No, this isn't an astounding accomplishment to be proud we have progressed beyond, but more than one holy text says people can (and should) stone them. Sometimes we must take inventory and understand how far we've come.

In doing this, we reveal the biggest problem with universalism in the human experience: it's fake. *It's something we just made up to describe shit we see, just like everything else.* As both science and culture evolve, both naturally and because of the increased flow of information, little holes like that get poked in what is generally accepted as "universal" truth. People begin to question things. Some of those things stop being holy.

As inconsistencies make it harder to accept these ideas at full bore, we search for replacements. Some try other religions and find what they're looking for; others don't. While "enlightenments" have happened throughout the course of history, I want you to consider what the increased influence of the ideology of individualism has done to the approach of many people.

It's not that people have gone searching for a new God; it's that the old one became questionable. Critique and deconstruction strip the abstraction all away, but it has nothing to do with *dealing with the effects* of people scrutinizing universalist ideas. Yes, that our cultural norms have received this scrutiny is a good thing. I vastly prefer the Christians of today to the ones that enacted the Crusades. However, I think the system in which the deterioration of centralized, universalist religions happened made way for The Religion of Me.

Individualism is a brilliant concoction, though I'd like to remind you that "brilliant" is not necessarily good. Individuality is legitimate; we are all *definitely* individuals with different thoughts, dreams, and approaches, so it may seem like a good idea to build societal philosophy around that. But rather than accommodating and incorporating the differences we all have—our essence—into a diverse society, it functions more to isolate people from each other.

Philosopher Karl Marx wrote of the alienation a person feels from their "species-essence," or what it is to be human, which he believed was the ability to shape things around us with conscious intent. The work individuals' lives are made up of often has little to do with what truly matters to them. The individual does not feel as though they have much say in their situation, and individuals do not come together.

Earlier in the book, I mentioned I hate when people send me cat pictures to cheer me up. This is an example of something about me, individually, that totally isolates me from other people. I most likely have several subconscious reasons for disliking this. It is partially that it feels like allowing a photo of a cat to assuage my problems equates with avoiding them. Avoidance always feels like helplessness to me. But if I'm being honest with myself here, it's also probably partly a non-conformist act I'm pulling.

I, like all people, have been brought up to think I'm somehow intelligent for "resisting the programming, maaaaaaan." The weird thing is, there's always an alternate "program" that accommodates our resistance to whatever kind of lifestyle marketing that makes us queasy. For every action, there's an equal and opposite reaction. For every rebellious teen, there's a punk band on a label that isn't Warner Music, but it is *owned by* Warner Music.

Not that musicians don't make rebellious music or that their messages are automatically inauthentic, but their insurgence is compensated for by creating a culture of overconsumption based around it. Your food has to come from somewhere.

That identity can be used to create and nurture a dependence on new products and updates tied to the person, group or entity is what I want to bring up here. Capital cultivates people's identity with the intent of inspiring less scrutiny. A worldview where identity, individual expression, politics and enjoyment are rooted heavily in consumption creates an ever-expanding list of demands for profiteers to supply. To transform various competing aesthetics and attitudes into consumer goods not only serves to generate profit, but also to stop the progression of idea-based resistance to these exploitative modes of operation.

The choices we have access to regarding the lives we lead are not limitless, despite what we may be repeatedly told and even what it may look like. As demographics split into smaller and smaller micro-demographics, we are more specifically categorized and then presented different options to consume. There's a profile of every one of us on a server somewhere; hell, more than one. The information recorded there helps to determine what advertisements we are shown as we do anything online, as well as influences our search results on both traditional search and social content platforms like YouTube or Twitter.

But again, the insidious part: we're making our own choices and are therefore less likely to question what we are presented with. The customer is always right.

However, the right to choose doesn't mean the right to meaningful choices; as stated earlier in the book, choice is still choice even if prefabricated or co-opted. If an entity or institution can provide an experience that validates the consumer while keeping them on a controlled path, that person is dedicating their time to the enrichment of that entity or institution. Time, attention, and data are all forms of currency, and if one knows what to do with them, one can amass an amazing amount of power.

Through the years, "individualism" has been conflated with "individuality." I try to draw the distinction that individually is the acknowledgement that we are individuals with our own wants, needs and taste. Individualism sounds very much like it could be that, but it's not; it is an ideology.

Individualism itself is The Religion of Me, and it slots itself very well into the kind of "profit-seeking through environmental control" I've been talking about. To attempt to tell people about this, we must overcome a strong inclination to regard this as trickery. In my 20s, I would try to tell people they were being manipulated, but the response was always some variation of "I'm not. I make my own choices." People feel like being told they are being tricked is an insult to their intelligence. It's also just entirely incorrect. Like I said, it's the environment that's been engineered, not the individuals.

Because we're constantly encouraged to be *more* of a closed-off individual, we become more disenchanted with "the other side," and then eventually even the people with whom we ostensibly agree. In that we are meant to believe in ourselves, we have our own personal truths, therefore questioning what we perceive as our reality is seen as questioning *us*. This is a devastatingly bad proposition in a supposed meritocracy, where we must constantly be right and assume the role of "expert" in order to maintain the ability to make money in a world where entry-level jobs are exported or automated.

Individualism is an ideology and a philosophy. The bedrock of this belief set is the priority of the individual, that one's own desires and goals are the ultimate aspiration. The interests of the individual are given precedence over all other things. No social group is to have any kind of undue influence and any collective is the deliberate antagonist, for its stated purpose is the collective good and that supposedly interferes with the individual's plight.

I'm often criticized when I voice my distaste for individualism. People who do this tend to refer me to Max Stirner, a philosopher who supposedly has it all figured out. He wrote a book called *The Ego and Its Own* which was published in 1844.

What Stirner put forward in this book was that autonomy, or what I've been calling agency, is of the highest importance. He believed that the individual must free themselves from any and all external forces. This included ethics, ideology, other people, and even one's desires. He believed that "good" is basically synonymous with "unique." He was against all obligations, be they moral, political or familial. He didn't love "rational self-interest" and had his own definition for "egoism" that centered on autonomy, but like other definitions, I think the focus on the self as the ultimate authority is bunk.

To be fair to Max, he was right about the state (he was not a fan) and cleared the way for a lot of other important things. Existentialism and postmodernism have their roots in his work. Both ask vital questions that clear the way for what I'm doing in this book. Other important works that you can find Stirner's fingerprints on are Peter Kropotkin's *The Conquest of Bread* and Oscar Wilde's *The Soul of Man Under Socialism*, though I would say I think that both of their ideas on individualism trend toward simple anti-authoritarianism than Stirner's (or Rand's) "shed all influence and obligation, agency is the highest ideal and selfishness is good."

To follow Stirner's philosophy as a purist would require constant justification of the emotions one would feel. Frankly, to categorize familial responsibility as little more than a hindrance demands endless justification for love. It must meet the requirement of "not sacrificing autonomy" to be valid, which makes me think of Max Stirner in the context of the Reddit incel (an "involuntary celibate" person who seems to think the world owes them sex). To be in love with someone, however, is to care about them in a way that does obligate certain things. Truth, transparency, and even simply caring are obligations love brings, and I don't know too many people who would say "I don't want those things from another."

In Stirner's eyes, others are "nothing but my food, even as I am fed upon and turned to use by you." I'm not going to pretend this is a deep dive into Stirner, and you will absolutely find material of his that is useful.

But I cannot resist; if he weren't a Reddit incel, I think Stirner would have at least been some 4chan dipshit had he lived in this era (complete with ironic racism). To me, he comes off as a selfish man-child who happened to have some decent ideas about some things while endlessly shouting that he should be doing as he pleases always. This is the area of his work that I think today's individualism comes from.

Of the utmost importance to an individualist is opposing interference with the interests of the individual— from society or institution, public or private. This is often to such a degree that any kind of collective is characterized as totalitarian, either loosely or to the point they are synonymous. Ayn Rand's philosophy of objectivism really doesn't read that differently from *The Ego and His Own*. The focus is in different places, but I have sincere doubts Stirner would dislike *The Virtue of Selfishness: A New Concept of Egoism*.

When materializing these abstract concepts, we must understand there is a large amount of nuance. We can't and shouldn't advocate against free will, nor freedom of expression, but these concepts are also complex. Technically, killing someone is a form of expression, but we shouldn't really have the freedom to do that if we're calling ourselves "civilized," so that would mean "freedom" can't mean "unlimited freedom." It would eventually restrict itself through tyranny. Not that our current concept of "law" does a particularly good job of ensuring justice.

Not having some means of recourse would be very disturbing, but it's also very clear that law is abused. Stirner's answer was for the individual to reject all of that and allow for autonomy, which would most likely make "revenge" and "justice" seem a lot more similar. "An eye for an eye" is not something everyone has the stomach, means, and/or ability to do, though, so those who cannot would become ruled by those who can.

A word being thrown around in political arguments a lot is "tribalism," which is almost never regarded as a positive. Besides the issue that it creates possible negative connotations for indigenous tribes of people in framing the concept as a negative, there's also a lot of issues with what the word is used for. Often, it's used to describe a certain level of perceived conformity in a group of people. I also see it used regularly as the bogeyman in a binary where individualism is the hero.

My belief is that individualism *feeds into* the phenomenon people call "tribalism." I think "tribe," in this case, is basically referring to Stirner's "union of egoists." These act as groupings of similarly minded individuals which do not subordinate to the collective good of the group. You can probably guess, but they all retain agency and don't really act like a group. Instead, they act more as an association of individuals. You can see this in online "movements" that amount to "I don't like this thing and believe it should be attacked," like GamerGate, a movement that called itself a "consumer revolt." Instead of being individuals banding together to use collective power to demand the end of exploitative practices or to improve conditions through awareness, it was ultimately a conduit for people to validate their dislike of a changing social landscape.

A person doesn't generally wish to be totally alone in life and will often seek out companionship of some kind. I think the "tribalism" that's being referred to is specifically due to people being unwilling to acknowledge anything but themselves as inherently correct. They *must* associate with people who specifically reinforce their worldviews. I don't think it's conformity; I think it's mutual need for validation and attention that human beings inherently have.

However, when people who believe they are entirely correct about everything get together, there's eventually going to be problems. Because of this, there will, in due course, be in-fighting, because the foundation of the group is not based in the evolution of ideas and mutual respect; it's simply a lot of people who think they are right about everything and who happen to think the same thing. The prominent individuals among them are called leaders because their takes are the absolute *hottest of the hot* and they do a good job maintaining attention, but they're not developing the group's ideas philosophically—and neither is the group. Because of needs socialized in a society that is best described as "neoliberal capitalism," we often consume human interaction as one might with any product, and therefore we have certain expectations. Ultimately, the group is there to validate everyone involved. The customer is always right.

You'll notice I didn't associate this with a particular side of the political spectrum, and while I do think one side is guiltier of this than the other, I don't want you to think that I think it's just one. Hopefully, the ambiguity of "who" will get you to think about the structures and hierarchies *you're* involved in and whether they act this way to some degree.

These groups are not hive minds; they're shaky alliances. They aren't based in solidarity or common cause (even if they purport themselves to be); they exist to find validation through the metrics of a group. "Many people agree with me, so I must be right." The phenomenon I am describing is one of many things that feeds into "perpetual correctness," which I will detail later. Essentially, I don't think "tribalism" or "union of egoists" are good terms for this. In my view, they're more like "validation gangs."

We shouldn't try to end the idea of the individual, though; instead we need to end the idea that everything hinges on the individual.

Individual responsibility sounds like a good concept, and if you take it to mean "keeping your house clean or paying your bills," it is. I'm not talking about those things, though. Nor am I talking about your culpability in a crime or whatever thing you hear people bring up when talking about individual responsibility. What I'm talking about is *your situation.*

What we're dealing with is the idea that your situation is 100% *entirely* of your own doing. In a world based in what we're *referring* to as "individual responsibility," if you've done well in the world, it's because you've worked hard and did a good job. No systemic considerations should be made. There should be no talk of your privileges, any inherited wealth, or lack thereof.

The tradeoff of there being no systemic factors in your success is that your failures are also entirely your fault. If you don't succeed, you didn't try hard enough. You didn't work hard enough. You didn't bother to become educated.

If the individual is the prime actor in society, then it's your fault that you haven't seen all the information, despite the fact there's no reliable guarantee you'll ever get exposed to that information. There's also no guarantee that when given a choice, you will be given a good choice. You may never be exposed to a good option, and you'll be blamed for it *because you're ignorant.*

Being ignorant is a grave misdeed in the world of individual responsibility. How dare you.

This is how individual responsibility is used as an excuse to marginalize people who are different in some way, as well as perpetuate the myth that no matter what circumstances you're born into, all it takes is hard work to get out. If you compare the numbers of people who are working to the number of people living with no monetary worries, you'll see why it's popular to criticize "the 1%," who happen to hold more wealth as the bottom ninety percent.

In 2017, psychologists Nicole Stephens and Sarah Townsend published a research paper in the Harvard Business Review entitled "How You Feel About Individualism Is Influenced by Your Social Class." Their research draws a picture of two totally different perspectives:

> *Our body of ongoing research shows that people from working-class backgrounds tend to understand themselves as interdependent with and highly connected to others. Parents teach their children the importance of following the rules and adjusting to the needs of others, in part because there is no economic safety net to fall back on. Common sayings include "You can't always get what you want" and "It's not all about you"; values such as solidarity, humility, and loyalty take precedence.*

> *In contrast, people from middle- and upper-class contexts tend to understand themselves as independent and separate from others. Parents teach kids the importance of cultivating their personal preferences, needs, and interests. Common sayings include "The world is your oyster" and "Your voice matters"; values such as uniqueness, self-expression, and influence take precedence.*

But can you sell that stuff? Ayn Rand tended to hold production as an incredibly individualist trait. And if you aren't producing something, to Ayn Rand, you are a parasite of some kind. These amazing producers take their product to market. As Rand says in *The Virtue of Selfishness*:

> *An individualist is a man who lives for his own sake and by his own mind. He neither sacrifices himself to*

> *others nor sacrifices others to himself. He deals with
> men as a producer.*

But a market isn't just merchants. Customers must exist, and you know this already, but the customer is always right. Everything in today's America is meant to be a transaction, meaning you're always the customer and you're always right.

People like to negatively associate participation trophies with collectivism or equality, as if it is an expression of entitlement that all should have reward. But tell me something, are all those people sharing one trophy? Did the collective achieve a goal and collectively receive a reward? Is that one trophy for many? No, it's one trophy *per individual.*

A participation trophy is an instance of "the customer is always right." The event stops being about competition and starts being about the individual and their validation. Not that endless competition is the healthiest thing in the world, but it's the thing that sports are usually said to be about.

A participation trophy is the individual and their parents *consuming the event*. The event is a product—an experience. And it is the means to monetize all the individuals and their parents' *validation*. If you want to criticize participation trophies, talk about the commodification of experience and realize that it is capitalism and individualism. The event organizer buys the trophies and money is made.

Another of Ayn Rand's favorite things is acting in "rational self-interest." In her eyes, actions can only be rational or logical if they act in the interest of the individual performing them. Which sounds *pretty damn rational* until you consider that it was contextually used to undermine the idea of altruism. It doesn't really seem possible for absolutely everything to be altruistic and therefore it's not realistic to expect. But to act out of pure selfishness on an ongoing basis would likely be more destructive than thinking the people of the world should focus more on helping each other.

Selfishness does not benefit the many; it doesn't even benefit the few. It benefits the individual.

I believe selfishness to be utterly bunk as a guiding, primary societal virtue. Yet, we have a system that incentivizes it. If you're not putting yourself and your needs before other people and theirs, you often can't get anywhere. So, from the perspective of getting anywhere in capitalism, greed is good. However, as I said earlier, perspective is a very individual thing.

We've talked about both biological and cultural difference in perspective. Whereas someone from a poor background may not see the benefit in pure unchecked greed, Scrooge McDuck has already received it. I mean, do you know what swimming around in a pool of gold coins is like? Because I do not. People see things differently.

We talked about philosophers of the postmodern era having different things to say, but that ultimately a common theme is a rejection of empiricism and objective reality with the understanding that human perspective makes that impossible.

In perhaps the most amazing feat of irony ever, objectivism, Ayn Rand's philosophy, a philosophy that has guided some of the primary economic actors of modern society, including Alan Greenspan, one of the best known economists and former chair of the federal reserve, *also understands this*.

In fact, one of the central tenets of objectivism is that reality exists totally independent of human consciousness. Human beings only have contact with reality through perception. This really lines up with what we are talking about here, doesn't it?

However, where postmodernism uses this to frame critique of human perception, objectivism asserts that you can attain objective knowledge through perception and the

71

application of inductive logic. Though, I feel this is effectively self-aggrandizement.

Through a standardized process of scrutiny and acceptance evidence, we can create collective reality. This certainly requires more than one person's perception with a kind of logic that deals with more than probabilities and likelihoods. This is not just perception of an event or object, but their perception of the evidence regarding it. The more people who understand the historical and cultural implications in context of these things, the more likely our collective reality is to be internally coherent.

Which, by the way, accuracy is another human concept. It does not mean perfect. Perfect is impossible. Though, we seemingly demand perfection of everyone and everything, including ourselves and the ones we love.

The real irony, though, comes as one preaches the values of the individual and the philosophy of individualism mixed in with the attack *on individuals who are different from oneself.* This clear contradiction is a large part of why I believe the philosophy of individualism feeds into the concept of a custom reality rather than being a legitimately workable concept built around individuality. It often seems to me that people who believe in the individual over all else act as if their thoughts are then the only ones which are true. "It's not about what other individuals want! It's about what *I* want."

There's a difference in acknowledging the individual and claiming that individualism is the correct philosophy. But if I'm correct *(a vulnerable preposition on my part, in which I acknowledge I may not be)* about the effects of ideological implementation of individualism in the philosophical sense, it's one of the larger things responsible for the breakdown of reality in a manner that consolidates power among those that already have it.

In a speech back in 1975, Margaret Thatcher said the following:

We're all unequal. No one, thank heavens, is quite like anyone else however much the socialists may pretend otherwise. And we believe that everyone has the right to be unequal.

This takes advantage of our mass conflation of individuality and individualism, capitalizing on the framework of "inequality as uniqueness." It's brilliant in that respect; this works well to *stigmatize equality* as a conflicting concept that competes with individuality. However, "if everyone is equal and of equal standing, everyone would just be the same" is not a statement that would hold up to even minor scrutiny.

What must be said, however, is that all this criticism comes from *my* custom reality.

Because of the fragile nature of *anything* conceptualized by humanity, reality is a very fragile construct. Individualism and profit motive can combine to create deeply divergent, customized paths we can all choose to take on our own. If I do not acknowledge that this is *my perspective* on the problem of how we pushed reality to its breaking point, I'm not being intellectually honest with you.

I do, however, believe wholeheartedly in what I'm saying here. More importantly, I'm saying it in a genuine attempt to get us all on a path to a viable collective reality. But even though I acknowledge that I am a vulnerable, possibly incorrect human being, I'm going to pull a Disney's Aladdin here and reach out my hand to you.

Do you trust me?

PETER COFFIN

5. THE MARKETPLACE OF IDEAS

I am not a salesman. Yes, I very much want to persuade you to agree with me on the ideas I'm presenting and hope we can collectivize some or all of reality, starting with *what reality is*. But in acknowledging I *could* be incorrect, I effectively ended the ability for you to "buy it."

Sales is about overcoming objections and solidifying a product's purchase as a sound decision. It's also about hiding flaws and uncertainty. I don't wish to follow that process with you, because I'm not "selling" my ideas to you. At least not in any traditional sense; you already bought the book! LOL, right? I'm already cashing the check and buying an island whether you agree with me or not. I've gotten away with it!

I'm sorry.

Thing is, I don't *want you* to "buy it" in any metaphysical sense. I am not looking to achieve market share, nor am I looking to compete. I don't want a monopoly over your mind.

A controversial term recently used much more than in years past is "neoliberalism," meaning the application of the free market to literally everything. There's another philosophy that operates similarly called transactionalism, which openly posits that all interaction be considered transactional. Neoliberalism, while not exactly the same, shares a lot of the gross reductionism that would make a person view human interaction as a commodity or transaction. Indeed, the effects of neoliberalism feel very transactional.

Neoliberalism installs a market situation, economically speaking (as it would have to, since derived from liberalism, which can be defined very simply as "freedom through markets"). But it goes beyond that and employs markets as solutions in our social problems. If you've ever heard the term "social capital" used instead of "trust," "integrity," or "credibility," then, at least in my opinion, you've witnessed the effects of neoliberalism. There is a certain dehumanization that comes with framing social interaction as a commodity.

The need to marketize comes from three places: those who believe in market philosophy's tenets in their need for "fairness," those who are ignorant of market philosophy but still have a need for "fairness," and those with an excessive concentration of wealth. Make no mistake, the waters are very muddy as to who is who, but this gives us another lesson in perspective. If a system which people can game to hoard power seems fair to most other people, then it also seems fair that the grifters grift. You may have heard, but we got a President that way.

Marketizing the social sphere makes things needlessly hyper-competitive and encourages people to prioritize superiority and gaining power. Sound familiar? That's because this is how we do things.

Some who ostensibly support social justice do not care about economic justice. Some think the economy is unrelated and believe working specifically in the social sphere will change material conditions. These people are often good, and informed discussions about how social and economic injustice overlap usually do make a difference with them. Also, some others know that if we get to messing with the economic power structures too much, the following they have accrued by painting themselves as an activist "thought leader" would not be as useful in a monetary sense.

This is bound to make some people angry, but there are social justice advocates that are hard neoliberals (or cultural capitalists, if you will). These people make up a tiny minority of these movements, however, and are not a legitimate means of discrediting large numbers of people simply seeking equality. I'm not even asserting they are not serious about their stated cause, just that there's a side motive of personal enrichment that is enabled and encouraged by their ideology. Also, their rivals in the anti-social justice space are usually a lot worse about profiteering on what they assert to be their beliefs.

In neoliberalism, profit (both monetary and social) can be derived by saying what people want to hear. Social interaction and discourse are commodities. So how do we exchange them?

Well, that would be the Marketplace of Ideas, a notion that is touted as the means of facilitating the adoption of concepts through a metaphorical free market. Through this symbolic belief bazaar, it's proposed that the "truth" will, by default, emerge from the competition of ideas in the public discourse.

One of the earliest mentions of ideas competing in a societal market was in a court case between the US government and Jacob Abrams, an anti-imperialist who got in trouble with the US government (can't imagine why... okay, I can and it's because the US acts very imperialist). My interest in this case doesn't concern the specifics, but rather a dissenting opinion about the result written by Justice Oliver W. Holmes, Jr:

> *The ultimate good desired is better reached by free trade in ideas… The best test of truth is the power of the thought to get itself accepted in the competition of the market, and that truth is the only ground upon which their wishes safely can be carried out.*

This is a quote that has been extensively covered in many forms of media, garnering a large amount of support over the last century. The interesting thing, however, is that support for Mr. Holmes' idea isn't necessarily support for "The Marketplace of Ideas" itself. For instance, centrist (and huge Oliver W. Holmes, Jr. fan) Alan Dershowitz had this to say about it when he reviewed a book about Holmes called *The Great Dissent* for the *New York Times* in 2013:

> *The dissent introduced into American constitutional law Holmes's concept of 'free trade in ideas — that the best test of truth is the power of the thought to get itself accepted in the competition of the market.' This was an imperfect analogy, since ideas are not commodities traded on markets, like oil futures, stock shares or gold, which are appropriately regulated by government agencies.*

Thing is, the idea of "The Marketplace of Ideas" is what stuck. Though I can't imagine it a heavy deviation from what came before in the already-capitalist United States, American truth testing is done essentially through this framing of a competitive marketplace—apparently, to the dismay of Mr. Dershowitz. Though I will say, I believe that the net effect of "The Marketplace of Ideas" is essentially golden mean-oriented centrism like his own. Speaking of which, here's a quote from a Fox News article Alan wrote in 2017 entitled "Berkeley must defend Ben Shapiro's Right to Speak":

Ben Shapiro must not be prevented from speaking. His talk must not be cancelled, as others were. Berkeley must do whatever it takes to protect Shapiro and those who follow him from the intolerant mobs that don't want anyone to hear his conservative message. What is at stake is more than Shapiro's personal freedom of speech, important as that is. What is at stake is the right of every American to participate in the open marketplace of ideas. If a great university shuts down that marketplace, the rights of all Americans are endangered.

When it comes to centrism, I agree with this fairly widespread meme depicting "Fish Hook" theory:

FISH HOOK THEORY

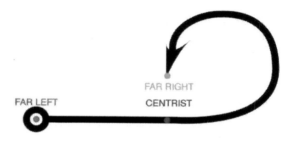

Like most, I was taught that the truth always prevails, that the best ideas are implemented, that working hard is all it takes to generate "merit," and that presenting a rational approach will make all the difference in the world. But if this were true, then ideas and ideology could very well actually have their validity derived from competition within this metaphorical market.

However, I haven't seen much of that during my time on Earth. What I said in the previous chapters on postmodernism and individualism regarding perspectives on words like "truth," "best," "rational," and "valid," as well as the consumptive situation that perspective is used to create, are precisely why a supposed marketplace of ideas cannot work in the way our society proposes it does.

If we understand that there is no "ultimate truth," but do not understand the need to collectivize reality and labor at maintaining it, we throw the deck up in the air, shouting "52 pickup!" This mixes harshly with systemic encouragement to regard ourselves as moral and intellectual authorities while obsessively consuming co-opted culture. With everyone operating in their own reality, consensus is not just unscientific, it's *coincidental.* I'm hardly the first person to make these kinds of assertions, too. The *Duke Law Journal* published a paper by Stanley Ingber entitled "The Marketplace of Ideas: A Legitimizing Myth" in 1984, the same year in which I was born, that makes the same assertions.

> *If truth is to defeat falsity through robust debate in the marketplace, truth must be discoverable and susceptible of substantiation. If truth is not ascertainable or cannot be substantiated, the victory of truth in the marketplace is but an unprovable axiom. In order to be discoverable, however, truth must be an objective rather than a subjective, chosen concept.*

For truth to be determined through a marketplace model, *fact must be objective.* I have been saying, as many have before me, that it is not. Recall that simply because a person's vision might be slightly blurrier than someone else's, these two people perceive things differently. They occupy the same space, but their "personal truth" is different. One person sees a very detailed object and can discern fine differences, while the other may only know it by its outline.

Again, if there were no humans in the universe, the universe would still exist, though "facts" would not. We made up "facts." People came up with the concept of fact and therefore it is inescapably human. It is imperfect, just as all of us are. Ingber continues:

> *Consequently, socioeconomic status, experience, psychological propensities, and societal roles should not influence an individual's concept of truth. If such factors do influence a listener's perception of truth, the inevitable differences in these perspectives caused by the vastly differing experiences among individuals make resolution of disagreement through simple discussion highly unlikely. And if the possibility of rational discourse and discovery is negated by these entrenched and irreconcilable perceptions of truth, the dominant 'truth' discovered by the marketplace can result only from the triumph of power, rather than the triumph of reason.*

Ingber posits that for the model to work, different positions in society shouldn't affect people's perception of truth. Remember the Harvard Business paper about how individualism is viewed differently by socioeconomic position? That's people viewing *even the idea that they view things differently* in different ways.

Reality has different demographics. To some, the best way to solve the problem of climate change is to "just stop talking about it" because "it's more of that libtard shit." The "truth" doesn't automatically have anything to do with scientific consensus, but rather being "rational" by someone's individual definition of the word. Let's also not forget this is a word often used disingenuously to uphold a status quo those in power find favorable. If one does not consider scientific research, either through intentional omission from worldview or simply through ignorance, then it's actually *pretty rational* to go outside in January and say, "it's cold, so climate change must be a hoax." Add in the choir of voices willfully using the conflation of weather and climate to justify environmentally dangerous action and it's sometimes hard to know where one stands.

The stated goal of a market is not a monopoly or any dominant situation; it's to provide a platform for competition, generating refinement and evolution of products. This would supposedly end in multiple choices for the "consumer," all of which have been continually improved upon with the hope of winning over customers based on merit. If the Marketplace of Ideas worked like this, we would never actually choose which ideas are fact… so it kind of works like this. *Kind of.*

The actual result of a free market, however, seems to generally be a monopoly, a duopoly, or an oligopoly; competition slows down and differences are expressed in brand image more than in product specs. Eventually, the biggest always eat the others. For instance, there are only six media conglomerates in the United States of America and the mergers haven't stopped. In theory, someone could eventually own all media, though there are laws that will supposedly stop that. This is basically how the Marketplace of Ideas is *purported* to work; there is a "winner," eventually.

Somewhere in between these two situations is how the Marketplace of Ideas actually works. We do choose some facts to be real, but they are often the two opposing facts that are most popular, creating a situation with only a few dominant forces. Those contradictory facts can never be decided upon in any finality; they must engage in unending competition. I think the market framework encourages this, and therefore discourages any kind of collective finality on an issue.

The only way something can change is that once an issue becomes viable, both economically and socially, our neoliberal capitalist constructs deem it worthy enough to attempt to provide products, services, and solutions for its realization. None of this is permanent, either, and can only last if a majority accepts it as reality. My favorite examples are renewable energy and marriage equality. Now that they're both considered valid and make money, you see Exxon investing heavily in renewable energy (though ceasing almost none of their still-profitable oil operations) and wedding cake shops specifically catering to gay couples (except at least one run by a homophobe). Never mind that over 95% of the scientific community has been talking about climate change for 40+ years. Never mind that gay people are *human beings and should therefore have the same rights as other human beings.* There's criteria, damn it! Polls!

Many personalities, both conservative and liberal, will happily bring up the Marketplace of Ideas to defend the speech of people like climate change deniers, anti-vaccine activists and race realists. This is because regardless of how socially progressive someone is, liberalism is inseparable from the free market; it was originally conceived of with "liberty through markets" as a foundational principle. The attitude embodied in a quote constantly attributed to Voltaire (but one he never said) is on display: "I don't agree with what you say but I will defend to the death your right to say it."

A liberal would rather see a "great debate" with a Nazi than for someone to punch them as they continue to work towards genocide. This is because their belief is that the Great Idea Market will automatically compensate for the Nazi's horrible ideas, and individual people will happily accept the rational argument provided by their opponent, regardless of previous position and environment.

One could say this comes from a position of elitism, in which they believe that they simply *know more* than the Nazi. A smart person could never become a Nazi! So, they will show their intellectual superiority in a battle royale. The liberal spectacle of the "showdown debate" is a bit of a perversion of discourse, but an interestingly fitting one. What's the point of a prize fight? For the organizers to make money. Showdown debates like the ones CNN holds to with Ted Cruz and his binders of "helpful statistics" that show us why healthcare is impossible amount to treating what should be reserved for exercising scrutiny as a sporting event, one where headlines the next day can talk about how much one "eviscerated" the other. That gets clicks! The "obviously good" opinion gets to show how superior it is to the "obviously bad" opinion, and obviously that's all it takes. Hard to do that if those "dummies" don't get to advocate for genocide.

The idea that "destroying" them on TV stops this kind of ideologue or what they advocate for isn't how things work. When a white supremacist is given the platform to say their piece, people sympathetic to that belief (or prone to be) galvanize. Many find they are not alone; this white supremacist, on TV no less, has validated the viewer's questionable worldview, something maybe no one else in their life does. This is the beginning of a validation gang.

In the meantime, the consensus may very well be that what the Nazis are saying isn't good. There's a problem in this, though: if consensus isn't automatically scientific, determining what is fact by simple consensus is a logical fallacy, in my opinion one of the logical fallacies that matters more. It's specifically called "the consensus fallacy," but it goes by other names, too. For instance, *argumentum ad populum*, "appeal to popularity," or simply a "bandwagon." This is the kind of collective reality that I think sucks ass.

Though, one must keep in mind science is also a human construct and therefore isn't perfect. There's a reason not to simply believe that "if we just do science everything will be fixed!" There is a phenomenon known as the replication crisis—the results of many scientific studies, new and old, are impossible to replicate (or nearly so). This is found when researchers, either an inquiring mind or the original researcher, wish to place more scrutiny on scientific findings.

For instance, the entire concept of an "Alpha Male" was first conceptualized by Rudolph Schenkel in the 1940s, but was most popularized by a book published in 1970 by L. David Mech entitled *The Wolf: Ecology and Behavior of an Endangered Species*. In it, he makes the same case that had been made before, that one wolf becomes dominant and leads the pack. This idea came from observing wolves in captivity, which was also where prior assertions came from. But wolves do not naturally live in captivity, and these behaviors did not repeat in observation of wild wolves. In the years following the publishing, he disavowed these dominance hierarchy dynamics. The original results are not repeatable in a real world situation.

The crisis here is one of verification. Scientific verification requires the ability to repeat the results of a similar experiment, and organizations don't accept results without a lot of rigid controls and requirements. This has been agreed upon by many (not all) people who are constantly trying to prove and disprove assertions made with this same method. This is *not* how a market works. If anything, a market is an institution where you, the individual (or whatever entity ends up being the customer), will decide if you "buy it."

This is the polar opposite of universalism.

It's important to specify that scientific methodology is not universalist; nothing created or observed by an imperfect human mind is. It is, however, collectivist in practice; it sets standards we all agree on and, although there are indeed scientists that anonymously admit to falsifying information in studies, it's only two percent of them. It allows us to do everything we can as imperfect beings to find an educated "best guess."

It's reasonable to operate on assumptions found by agreed-upon methodology that have been checked by multiple people using the same methodology (not that it is a guarantee anything has). It is also reasonable to question these results if evidence is considered; revisiting assumptions is not inherently bad. The issue that an endless idea competition is not that any human assumption is infallible, but rather that previous evidence is ignored to prolong the conflict.

There's a propensity to argue against scientific consensus with popular consensus, particularly within whatever group is making an argument. Climate change is regarded as sound science, but some groups of people validate each other into believing it's nonsense. So, for the sake of clarity, when I mean consensus reached by science I will say "scientific consensus," and for societal/popular/group consensus, I will simply say "consensus."

A huge problem with the Marketplace of Ideas is that because it encourages fact-by-consensus, it's self-validating. There appears to be a consensus that the Marketplace of Ideas itself is valid, and even that it's somehow related to "freedom." I think this is an interesting manifestation of liberalism's "freedom through markets." This continually validates the entire concept by its own circular logic.

Scientific consensus does not share this trait with plain ol' consensus. At its best, science continues to test and retest, and it continues to do it with rigid methodology. This is not to say science is always at its best. When people don't adhere to this methodology, they are often discredited by individuals and organizations *who simply have to point out the lack of methodology*. When something isn't peer-reviewed, you can't just say that it is and walk off. People check you and they check your results. True, there is most certainly profit incentive to fake results. But unlike in a lot of other industries, there is at least some kind of baked-in scrutiny.

I'll be happy to acknowledge all the flaws in the reliance of human beings in either scientific or plain Jane consensus. However, I want to point out that the environment is relatively more accepting of incorrect assumptions. In many cases, incorrect assumptions have produced incredibly useful results. Some of the most useful inventions we use today were accidents, like microwaves and pacemakers.

Relatively speaking, as long as you were honest in reaching your conclusions, it is okay to be wrong in science. This changes the dynamic of defense by quite a bit; someone who has made an assertion in good faith and is proven wrong through honest means will look ridiculous if they do not back down.

It's fairly easy to pick out the hacks from the scientists. Andrew Wakefield, forerunner of the anti-vaccine movement, will not back down on his assertions despite having a near-endless stream of peer-reviewed, repeatable studies produce results that discredit his. There are literally hundreds to choose from; you could write a book filled with only citations of reproducible studies that debunk Andrew Wakefield. Still, he will not acknowledge that his methodology was flawed, and intentionally so. He will not state that he had financial incentive to produce the result that he did, but I'm sure lawyers that hired him to aid their lawsuit against a vaccine company paid him very well. Wakefield didn't get to continue as a scientist or doctor; he was stripped of his license to practice medicine and within the scientific community is *totally* discredited.

Unfortunately, consensus, even when scientific in nature, doesn't just automatically convince its own opposition. Wakefield isn't a doctor anymore, nor is he acceptable as a citation in academic circles, but he didn't do anything against the law, so he continues to operate as a businessman. Business is booming, too. The Marketplace of Ideas doesn't require peer review; in fact, any attempt to impose any regulatory consideration to *a metaphor* would likely be laughed at. On top of that, it's just not possible to shed disproven (or bigoted) arguments when the accepted mode of discourse extends them well beyond conclusion by continuing to platform opposition to scientific consensus. So, it's not only self-validating, it's self-perpetuating.

While this is not ideal for the stated purpose of the Marketplace of Ideas, it is indeed ideal for profit-seekers and agenda-pushers. Often, these are one and the same; see Wakefield. By presenting a disproven, bigoted, or otherwise silly viewpoint on a high-profile platform, one can become the leader of a validation gang. This position is a very easy one in which to generate revenue.

The Marketplace of Ideas doesn't work. At least, it doesn't work for its *stated* purpose.

When you have a horse in the race, you want that horse to win. That's the flaw in physical markets, as much as it is in this metaphorical one. Capital, systemically speaking, doesn't genuinely "want" a competitive situation where they're forced to evolve their products to be better than the other entries; they want market share so they don't have to deal with that shit anymore! They want to win and drive a Bugatti!

When we commodify something, we ensure its gamification. What I mean by that is commodification of ideas has led to the need (or perhaps just desire) for measurement. Inevitably, performance metrics lead to a "who's bigger" competition, whether explicit or implicit. This ultimately colored what we fondly called "the democratization of media" not so long ago.

At any point, you can post an idea on Facebook, Twitter, YouTube, or any number of other networks. What happens next? Well, it might get retweeted, liked or shared. Every time it does, the little number next to the button goes up. As it goes up, it's more and more likely to *keep* going up. Metrics that are generated, whether it's a tweet, a status update, or a video are a measurement of action on your idea.

The more often you can get high numbers next to those little icons, the more likely you will continue to get more. Gradually, we're conditioned to regard the blue thumbs up, the red heart, the green... retweet thing(?) with *respect*. Though I disagree with the concept, societally, these numbers signify credibility and the accumulation of "social capital."

As with the market itself, the want to measure self-validates and self-perpetuates. It becomes something of a thrill to see a surge in metrics, releasing endorphins into one's system and giving the satisfaction of knowing we're right once again. We're justified in doing the thing we did to see that surge (no matter how "good" or "bad"), and you may find that more people are willing to throw their lot in with you, for you have validated them.

The scary thing about the perspective of "I win because metrics. Neener neener" is that metrics can be gamed. If you want 50,000 YouTube views, there's bots for that. You could set them up yourself or you could pay someone who programs them to send a bunch of views your way. You can run challenges or giveaways that encourage people to engage with your content, or you could just advertise somewhere.

The fact that these things influence how many people see your idea or thought puts people who already have accumulated wealth and power at an advantage. It also makes success difficult to achieve without strong support. While "out" white supremacists are certainly a minority, several of them have accumulated vast wealth and many have relatively large validation gangs. This means they do have the advantage of the power to buy exposure as well as strong support. You can spend to make.

On the other hand, by all accounts I could find, trans people make up a tiny percentage of our population. Though some may have support structures and others may not, they don't have massive corporate money pushing in-depth trans content into the media or small doses of new information in memetic form. Often, content about trans people on anything but trans-owned media comes off as a pat on the back to the outlet, the consumer, and the author themselves for not being a monster. Much less seen are the studies and data-driven analysis regarding the issues trans people face in our world.

Yes, you see it on trans-owned media, but you rarely see a trans person on a major media outlet fielding anything but the most basic of good-faith (but still a bit ignorant) questions or grinning and bearing bad-faith criticism. Almost never is anything substantial done to normalize trans people. I'd say this is evidence that society has issues morally speaking, and that there isn't really any money in normalizing the actual humanity of trans people, but there's clearly money in asking white supremacists their opinions on things.

One way the Marketplace of Ideas works exactly like a real free market in every way is that it's flexible. It has no morals, ethics or code of conduct. Though, because it's not a real market, there's also no way to regulate it and therefore it basically just does whatever. It has no process, nor does it have any accountability. It's simply an abstract framing of how discourse works—one that gives us the impression we should approach discourse as a marketplace—through the lens of commodification and gamification. When we have an idea, we must act like business people to achieve anything with it.

This is a big part of what I believe to be the way to exploit said discourse, and if you can control the means through which we accept ideas on the societal level, you control the environment that we make our choices in and therefore our reality. There's no question of accepting the control itself, but, instead, the endless diverging questions about validity that everyone thinks they have the correct answer for.

I brought up trans content and white supremacist content because they perfectly exemplify the kind of imbalance I'm talking about: white supremacists raise insurmountable amounts of money to spend in the media, and trans people don't. They *can't*. Because of the social and economic disadvantages that come with being in a marginalized group, trans people have significantly more to deal with just to live some semblance of a normal existence. It's harder to organize a trans group because it's harder for someone who can't get a job due to covert or unconscious bias to show up to meetings or dedicate their time in other ways. People who worry about eating or where they'll sleep tonight can't spend the kind of time necessary to raise money for a cause—even their own.

White supremacists can raise money simply by dog whistling on a prominent platform. Old rich white dudes are going to send in money. Young white heirs to fortunes can also quite possibly be racist.

The Martel Society is a "paleoconservative," white nationalist, 501(c)(3) nonprofit group that was named for Charles Martel, who "held back a Muslim invasion of Europe by winning the Battle of Tours in the year 732," as stated by their promotional material. William Regnery II, heir to the publishing fortune that caters to far-right readers, founded the group in 2001. Regnery is called a "prime mover and shaker in white nationalism publishing," by the Southern Poverty Law Center, a group that tracks racism, along with other types of bigotry and extremism.

Ron Robinson and James B. Taylor are board members of several political organizations, first and foremost Young America's Foundation (YAF), one of the co-founding organizations that created the Conservative Political Action Conference (CPAC). Additionally, Robinson is on the board of Citizens United (yes, *that* Citizens United) and the American Conservative Union (which operates and administrates CPAC). These are extremely mainstream political organizations; CPAC itself is typically covered by the most prominent news outlets—conservative and otherwise. In 2017, former executive chair of Breitbart, Steve Bannon's speech at CPAC was broadcast live on several of these networks, including Fox News and CNN.

But Robinson and Taylor's activities don't stop there. They're also on the board of "America's PAC," an organization that has raised millions of dollars which it has both spent on various conservative political candidates and donated to conservative political organizations. One of those organizations is William Regnery II's Martel Society, the "paleoconservative," white nationalist nonprofit I mentioned earlier. America's PAC has sent thousands of dollars their way.

Trans people don't typically have heirs and board members of powerful, mainstream, political organizations funneling money into the media for them, but white nationalists do.

To be entirely fair, yes, there are a few PACs dedicated specifically to transgender issues. They are, however, not numerous. The first PAC dedicated specifically to trans issues, the Trans United Fund, was founded in 2016, but to call it a mainstream organization would be an overstatement of its influence.

This is but a tiny slice of what kind of money goes into getting ideas to "the market." To me, this makes the idea that "everyone has to be heard" seem very much like an illusion or perhaps an excuse. We see people say, "but everyone has to be heard" as they're pocketing money for airtime or advertisements, or even worse, funding "alternative media" organizations that traffic in "alternative facts" with the intention of profiting from misinformation.

Now, independent media isn't automatically bad, but it certainly isn't automatically good, either. If it's calling itself "alternative" media at this point, though, I'd be wary. That's a loaded term, not simply meaning "an alternative." This is a lot like what "indie" meant for a while in pop music; it was short for independent and that only *really* means that no conglomerate owns the rights to it. But in American canon, "indie music" has a specific sound.

The thing is, while I am essentially deriving my definitions of these things from their cultural significance, there are people who will sometimes stick to their dictionary definitions—and sometimes not—to derail the conversation. Someone will say "alternative media is just a choice to avoid the mainstream," and technically, they aren't wrong. Combining the fact that culture is not something created by committee or through specific oversight (which I think is good) with the way we have framed the acceptance of ideas through a marketplace (which modifies the way we interact with absolutely everything), we've created a framework by which reality itself can be controlled without exerting any physical force. In this framework, providing choices that account for the likely actions of an individual begins to make more sense as a means to control outcome of choice.

The result of commodification and competition is fragmentation. The very last thing we want to end up fragmented is the perception of reality by individuals. But that's where we are, isn't it?

Indeed, money might get you an advantage in the Marketplace of Ideas, but to put this in role-playing game terms, it's a buff. It's an advantage or a privilege, one that makes the battle ahead easier. But it's not the endgame of your actions in this market. You're not competing for money, you're competing for market share. You're looking to gain control.

Some assert that validity itself into the currency that is exchanged in this market. I heavily disagree with that proposition; how valid something is has very little bearing on its position in this market. How good it is doesn't matter; good means different things to different people, especially in this individualized, market-based reality where "the customer is always right."

So, if money isn't the currency, and the stated currency (validity) isn't the currency... what is? What does an idea accumulate as it gains market share in the Marketplace of Ideas? What do people pay to "invest" in an idea within this market?

What non-fiat tender is being exchanged for furthering an idea you believe to be correct? For the answer, I'd ask that you *pay* attention as we continue...

PETER COFFIN

6. ATTENTIONOMICS

Attention is currency in the Marketplace of Ideas. Now, if you had an actual, physical elephant in your room for five years, it wouldn't be weird to you anymore. Sure, it would be weird for someone else, but you've built routines around the damn thing at this point. It isn't coming out of your house unless you literally tear that corner of the structure out. If you do that, it's going to be one of those projects you never got around to finishing. Home renovation doesn't exactly cost peanuts. Peanuts do.

So, you're feeding it, cleaning up after it, and you know what? You're used to the smell. You didn't put the elephant there and no one's happy about it (least of all the elephant), but at this point you're doing what you can to keep yourself and the pachyderm alive.

Since this circus-dwelling shit machine demanded your attention for so long, it became normal. I don't think there is a complicated process in which conflicting information interacts to create a "hypernormal" situation. I don't think confusion is an element in it. I think you just do shit for a long enough time and people think it's normal. Do weird shit for long enough and people expect it. Doesn't matter if it's Tom Green, Lady Gaga, or Vladislav Surkov.

A good history and critique of reality comes in the form of Adam Curtis's 2016 documentary series, Hypernormalization. I do think it's a great series, though I believe there are certain concepts Curtis overcomplicates. He asserts that a lack of ideas to fix the USSR's counterintuitive, top-down approach to a system designed specifically to distribute power evenly, combined with constant dissemination of contradictory information by the state, caused a new kind of normality where the obviously false felt real, at least on some level.

I don't think that's why people accepted it, though. My characterization is much simpler: the USSR was just a shitshow for such a long time, it became normal. That's not to say I outright disagree with the film. I find a very large amount of it valid and the historical account it provides is nothing short of terrifying. I just think things are much simpler: whatever maintains attention becomes normal, *and normal is profitable*.

The USSR was not "evil." It was the product of a group of people who had, very specifically, fair ideology. There are issues with their implementation that made it susceptible to the issues of the very systems they were against, though. Where they sought economic equality, they believed this could be achieved by force of authority rather than by willful (and careful) building of horizontal, democratic hierarchy. I'm not someone who's going to demonize the USSR, but I disagree with how they went about doing things. It was a shitshow.

If something can get attention, there will be people who agree and people who don't. If those people clash, the ideas will get more attention. As this happens, they may be talked about in social, independent, or maybe even traditional media. Which will result in *(you guessed it)* more attention. The attention will give rise to the acquisition of *more attention*, and the longer the ideas can maintain this hypothetical mainstream attention, the more likely they are to be considered normal, and therefore increasingly called "correct" by a lot of people. And as previously said, value can be extracted from this process.

An idea that has become profitable in attention currency is primed to generate profit in fiat currency. This is why companies like Unilever piggyback on things like feminism to sell soap through their subsidiary Dove: feminism is relatively normal. Many women seem to support it anyhow (can't imagine why) and there isn't really much risk in supporting something that's normal. They also obviously consider "white" to be normal, which is why Unilever sells skin whitening cream in other countries. If someone's feminism is okay with that, I'm not okay with that person's feminism. Though I would say a corporation is not capable of caring about equality in any possible way beyond the most surface level.

To someone in the United States who has seen a Dove commercial a few times, it may seem normal that their soap is somehow associated with equality. This might cause them to purchase or to avoid the soap, because they might personally agree or disagree with that (there's also an identity-oriented aspect we will discuss later). The result will have been higher sales than simply attempting to sell soap on effectiveness, though, as there's not a lot of soap on the market that flat-out just doesn't work. It's the brand that matters, which includes the logo, the shape, the smell, and what the company wants to associate itself with. "Good soap" is not a description of effectiveness, it's a description of what someone feels about soap.

The point I'm making is that *facts don't automatically get attention*, which is the path to normalization or "share of the Marketplace of Ideas." This is why fact-checking doesn't really do much. Facts can certainly be interesting, but *are not automatically so*. Nothing is automatically interesting, fact or fiction.

This assertion is often met with one or both of two responses. The first is that we should put more work into making facts interesting. The second is that "people are idiots with the attention span of a gnat." Neither of these responses are based on a systematic assessment of the issue; the second blames individuals for the environment created by those in power and their predecessors, while the first blames facts for not being sound bites.

When fact is approached scientifically, the result is scientific consensus; I would call this a "good" form of collectivism. It's imperfect, but when executed in good faith is as close to perfect as humanity can be. Scientific consensus is process-tested, peer-reviewed and *proven*. Attempts to disprove it fail. In short, it takes a long time to reach scientific consensus, and it's often a cacophony of information coming together in conflict. The loose ends get tied up, but the road there can be frustrating and uncomfortable.

This process isn't something you'd make into a TV show. It's not that "facts are boring," but facts are often formed by findings presented years apart in studies and papers hundreds of pages long, not written by someone who cares if a lay person can understand. In fact, they might even hate us lay shit-eaters!

If collective fact was automatically an attention-getting concept, Donald Trump could have never won in 2016. Also, collective fact isn't just competing for attention, it's also competing with "alternative" (individualized) facts. Remember, the customer is always right! Given collective fact has a lot to deal with and is at a disadvantage for pretty much all of it, it doesn't make a lot of sense to run a political campaign on collective fact.

Alternative facts make the individual feel comfortable in the idea they are right. We're really going to dive into this in the next chapter, but I'd wager that doesn't sound too wrong, even without much explanation. If an alternative media source confirms the thing you believe, you at least give them more of a chance. Right?

Oh, come on! You do.

Let's say some things out there just gets *all* the attention. Donald Trump had a kid with Kim Kardashian who was then the *drunk* getaway car driver for a crime OJ Simpson and Tonya Harding committed in Hell, MI. Not only is their getaway car the Oscar Meyer Wienermobile, but during the police chase, Don and Kim's kid came out as gay via a drunken rant over the Wienermobile's built-in loudspeaker, jeopardizing their new sponsorship with Chick-Fil-A. It's the only news story for six months. That thing is in control, right?

If you have a ton of money, does that automatically mean you're in control? *Potentially.* That said, you aren't really in control if you don't know what to do with that money. To really exert some control, you need to set things in motion with that money. You need to pay some people to talk and some people not to. You need to get your message into living rooms. You need to forge connections and networks, to find people who do things that make your goals easier. In short, the money is the means. If you don't know what to do with it, you might as well not have it. The only thing having a ton of money automatically means is you can easily lead a comfortable life.

Attention is very similar. You can't just get attention and hope shit works out; you need a plan. Currency is a means, not an end. If you think it is an end, you will never get what you want out of it and thus will always seek more.

So, who controls the narrative in the bizarre situation I described earlier? Well, it's something that no one involved in planned to be public, so the originators of the story have already lost control of it. Where's the next bottleneck?

The media is *usually* the default controller, because they are the ones capable of attracting the most attention to a person, place, event or other thing. The way they present it is often the largest number of people's first impression; therefore, they get to dictate the input. What they present as fact is then accepted or denied by individuals and an opinion is formed—the Marketplace of Ideas!

We have two points of interest here. First, the mainstream and the alternative media alike are more than happy to misrepresent things in order to appease the demographic of which they are looking to secure the attention. The inherent credibility of a professional aesthetic (professional graphics, everyone has a suit, etc.), a lot of what they are saying, is taken as "serious" and that's what they care most about. Second, individuals are constantly given many variants on this call to action: "you've heard all the facts, now it's up to you to figure out what to believe." This ensures the company is not interfering with the agency of the person viewing, but we must remember that the outlet has already framed the facts through the bias that they believe will benefit the outlet best. After all, it's a business.

The decision to accept a media outlet's version of a story only seems like an individual exerting power until one considers the profit motive of such an outlet. Fox News is the easiest to figure out; it's a conservative news outlet and blatantly so. Their business model revolves around reinforcing the biases of people who have made the choice to be conservatives. No one else matters, so there is no incentive to consider outside viewpoints. They make money because people are conservatives, so it makes sense to encourage them to stay conservative. You can't *make* people do that, but you can curate an environment that feels satisfactory, as well as discredits criticism.

CNN is less obvious, because their political bias is center (center-left at times, but not too far in that direction), so it is not the stark opposite of Fox News. CNN used to be "the news network" and to garner a very utilitarian reputation for covering news and events from about as neutral a point of view as is possible for a corporation. The bias they're catering to isn't necessarily as overtly partisan, but rather the idea of hyper-awareness and savvy: everything they cover is presented as extremely important and vital to give attention to and, therefore, if you know what CNN is talking about, you're perceptive and knowledgeable. The bias they cater to is the idea that "I'm plugged in, I have my finger on the pulse of society." Everything on CNN is Breaking News—you *have to* know about this!

MSNBC is basically Fox News for liberals (like how conservatism is just liberalism for people who *automatically* hate immigrants).

They make money by maintaining an audience that is comfortable with the way things are being presented. In that comfort, when a commercial is aired, they are more likely to listen to what an advertisement says. You'll notice these outlets don't do much investigative reporting on companies that advertise with them.

When an outlet that gets lots of attention exhibits one of these biases, spending time framing their facts and arguments through a lens that will help them achieve their goal (profit), that's them directing the attention they get. This is the actual power of attention-as-currency. If you don't understand the necessity to do this that capitalism creates, you can't get market share in the Marketplace of Ideas. As said earlier, it's not about what is genuinely most valid. It's about what gets the most attention.

Attention itself can be controlled via platforming (or not doing so), but if you don't control the framing and flow of information, it's more likely you got rich by winning the lotto. However, in this scenario, you're one of those lotto winners you see in the news who goes bankrupt very fast because they have no idea what to do with that currency.

The ability to profit, both in social and economic context, means the goal of a situation *will always eventually be* profit. Maybe at first, people take it seriously. However, it becomes apparent that the ones who more clearly set their sights on profit go on to achieve it. For that reason, there's no incentive to push for equal representation of opposing ideas because that would give an observer the ability to consider both opposing ideas after having heard both arguments—you have no control over this situation. But if, as is implied by the name, the Marketplace of Ideas is a competitive market situation, that's what people would seemingly want. These inherently contradicting motives ensure nothing can ever be standardized, and therefore nothing can ever be decided.

Also, when one idea is represented more than another idea, that idea becomes "normal" or "acceptable," this means that it has won on at least some level, though not on one in which the competition is totally vanquished. If attention, the specific currency of this market, can be achieved by simply being louder than the competition, reaching people first and drowning out opposition, why wouldn't you do it that way?

Media is the *default* controller, but that can be overridden. When another source disseminates information in a controlled fashion, this may very well dictate the input. For instance, if someone says something that is questionable when without proper context, it could be sent to media outlets in a manner that said context isn't ever seen. The media outlet may sense profit in outrage and roll with it. Yes, the media would likely exert some degree of control over what is presented, but they are the secondary controller, not the primary one.

Similarly, a press release for a new product or service would never contain anything negative about the thing it wishes to promote. Can you imagine if Pepsi introduced a new drink saying "40% of our taste testers disliked it!" No, they'd say "the majority of people who tried it *loved it!*" If that press release is platformed (it usually is) and gains attention, as well as not being scrutinized heavily, that drink will probably sell well, at least initially.

When an idea's representation gets the bulk of the attention, that idea has a share of the market.

There's another exploit for the Marketplace of Ideas and its attention economy. We're about to talk about the two years of events that culminated on November 8th, 2016, so if you're not interested in Donald Trump, stop reading here.

You didn't stop reading there. Why are you reading more?

The truth is, you're interested in Donald Trump. I am too. How can anyone not be? Nothing about him is acceptable, yet he won *the Presidency*. He doesn't fit into a legitimately civil society, he's continually damaging cultural norms, and he's lied many times *to the people who put their faith in him*, yet many people think he's the most honest politician who's ever lived.

I'm interested in not having this kind of prolonged mess anymore and that doesn't just mean Donald Trump. Conditions led to Donald Trump. He is not the beginning of our problems, he's just the guy who lied most interestingly about how to solve them.

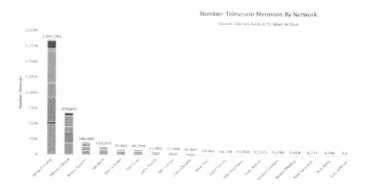

A tally kept by the Internet Archive TV News Archive kept track of media coverage the top 22 presidential candidates all got. Donald Trump received more than double the coverage Hillary Clinton got, who received double the coverage of Bernie Sanders, and no one else matters if you're going by this metric. In addition, it must be said that though Bernie Sanders did manage to force the media to cover him at times, the only people the media *really* cared about were Donald Trump and Hillary Clinton—and they cared about him twice as much as her.

Bought Versus Free Media

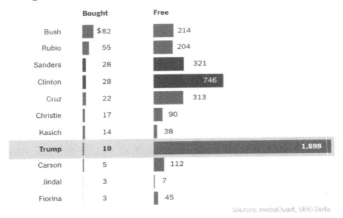

	Bought	Free
Bush	$82	214
Rubio	55	204
Sanders	28	321
Clinton	28	746
Cruz	22	313
Christie	17	90
Kasich	14	38
Trump	10	1,899
Carson	5	112
Jindal	3	7
Fiorina	3	45

Sources: mediaQuant, SMG Delta

If you looked at a study conducted by mediaQuant, a metrics firm, entitled "$2 Billion Worth of Free Media for Donald Trump," you'd probably be able to guess that most of the coverage Donald Trump got was totally free. He paid for roughly 0.05% of the coverage he received; at the time of the study, he had paid for a bit less than $10 million worth of coverage. If the media had charged him for all the free time he got, they would have sent him a bill for about $1.9 billion. By the *start* of the general election, Hillary Clinton had paid for about three times as much coverage ($28 million), and received about $746 million in free coverage. She effectively spent three times as much and got only 40% in return.

In a similar mediaQuant study entitled "A Media Post-Mortem on the 2016 Presidential Election," done after the election, the final estimate for the free coverage Trump accrued was $4.96 billion compared to $2.6 billion for Clinton. Trump's total was higher than every single other candidate of any party combined.

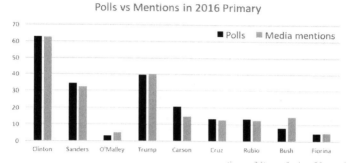

Polls vs Mentions in 2016 Primary

Nieman Lab at Harvard conducted yet another study entitled "Polls vs. Mentions in 2016 Primary," which, among some other things, considered the correlation between media coverage and pole position, finding the two are extremely closely tied. Now, to be fair, correlation doesn't equal causation. There is most certainly a degree of reaction within both sets of numbers. Polls likely influence who is covered and who is covered likely influences polls.

The ratios of poll position are *very similar*. The polls match the media mentions in every case except Jeb Bush, and that's likely because the amount of *paid* media coverage he received was significantly higher than everyone other than Hillary Clinton. Paid coverage appears to do less than an organic mention, though. Still, to see the numbers are as closely tied as Nieman Lab found should trouble you for more than one reason…

Well… "President Trump" is not hypothetical anymore. So, there's that.

The media just couldn't dictate the narrative with him. Since he managed to control what was said in essentially all coverage of him, while easily maintaining coverage at a rate no one was able to keep up with, Donald Trump overloaded the system. The overload allowed him to consistently reach people first with the version of information he wanted to be prominent. Covering Trump was ratings gold regardless of whether the viewers loved or hated him, so there was no profit motive to even really attempt to control these narratives. That's not to say the last few months they didn't try, but by then the circuitry was just too fried.

Donald Trump is hardly the first to do this; if you've ever dealt with GamerGate, been on the receiving end of organized attacks from channers or Kiwifarms, or have ever heard the term "lolcow," you know what I mean.

GamerGate started as a false story spread by the boyfriend of a game developer by the name of Zoe Quinn. It alleged that she slept with game journalists to get positive reviews of her game for profit. While at one point, she did date a games journalist, her game was free and entirely text-based. On top of that, these reviews don't exist. But if you mention any of this on social media, even today, a noticeable amount of people will approach you to tell you "what's really going on here." Their explanations range from mostly false to totally made-up, and I won't go into specifics. If you're interested in that incident specifically, Zoe Quinn has a book out about it.

This so-called movement was not without precedent; this should remind you of the way the far corners of the internet worked to spread disinformation about Anita Sarkeesian when she did a Kickstarter attempting to raise $6,000 for a new feminist series, but ended up raising over $200,000. When you mention her, people give you stories about how she's a scam artist in the hopes you take them at their word. There was also Retake Mass Effect 3, a movement that was basically the film Misery, except instead of a fan who tortured a writer because she thought the ending of a book was bad, it was many fans who tortured anyone and everyone who would listen to their whining about how the ending of a video game was bad. There were even positive things that came from these anonymous corners of the internet, like Project Chanology, a movement organized on and off image boards to expose Scientology as the dangerous organization it is.

These things vary in degrees of focus and seriousness. I know many people who were victims of the negative version of these kinds of campaigns, and I am also one. This simple fact is one of the bigger conduits for me organizing my perception of all this abstract thought.

Way back in 2007–2010, I was a somewhat popular YouTube sketch comedian. I still have the subscriber number to back that up. Though, the people who subscribed when they saw me on Annoying Orange tend not to watch me much anymore, now that I make documentaries, video essays on philosophy, and advertising critique. Who'd have thought!?

I was also in a relationship with someone who was misrepresenting who they were to me. Yes, I was catfished.

The way I interacted with this person was very public, and I didn't just start publicly having opinions about things recently. I voted for Barack Obama and supported a public option in the health care overhaul and was quite forward about all of that (as was I about my disappointment about all of it later). I also had the same distaste for many of the things I still have today, however, with less knowledge. In this instance, I had an issue with shady marketing targeting kids and teenagers, but I had not developed ideas on these things. So, I would make people angry because I would point at bloggers and YouTubers who were simply doing it and say, "BAD!"

That was messing with their money, though, and I probably should have had my house in order before criticizing people in ways that, on some level, threatened their livelihood. I was a nuisance with a weakness: an online girlfriend who was suspicious.

One of these personalities, a gossip blogger, did some digging and found out my catfish had been using photos of a celebrity in South Korea, a place I have very little knowledge of, least of all the language. Now, I don't know for sure what this blogger thought of me, but they published a blog post saying I made up a fake Asian significant other, so I could say racist things about Asians through this phony Twitter account that I was supposedly running, as well as not appear single. Only losers are single.

To this day, I have no idea if the blogger thinks that what they wrote is true or if they found inconsistencies in my life and knew it was enough to make it look as if I did this. I do get why they did it, though.

To summarize, I was an ostensibly well-liked internet personality with a following of people who listened to what I said and talked to other people as well. I was pointing out what I considered to be unsavory marketing to teenagers, but that was this blogger's income. If what I said gained any real attention, it would likely damage this person's ability to make money, even if just a little.

Anyhow, that post of hers spread along anonymous image boards, Facebook and LiveJournal. It then got back to a YouTuber—one could say *easily* the biggest at the time; one I had openly criticized for content theft on a regular basis and who still has me blocked on Twitter to this day—who decided to get the fly swatter out. He posted it to his Facebook page, where it somehow received over 77,000 likes. From here, it was picked up by Gawker and then everyone who used to mooch off Gawker.

This is not a narrative I had control over; the people dictating the input framed it in a way that established me as a pitiful, possibly racist, individual and the media itself simply repeated hearsay from gossip bloggers as "news." At this point, you should get why I have incentive to take these abstract progressions and figure out how to verbalize them.

Now, I don't want to prove anything to you. I have no agenda in explaining it other than to point out I have a horse in the race regarding your understanding of how what I claim to be false information about me became accepted as reality. I want you to know I have seen what I am describing first-hand and I have been at its mercy. I'm not the first person to experience such a thing, and I'm certainly not the one who's experienced it the worst. Marginalized people constantly receive this kind of treatment for no reason other than their identity.

But if I'm honest, at this point, I wouldn't change it. Would it have been nice not to live through that? Absolutely. I won't go into detail about what this caused me to lose, but I gained something that has paid off—understanding. "Getting it" was just impossible until this happened to me. It seems like none of this can really happen, but like I said, there are people who deal with nothing but this. There shouldn't be.

The Anti-Defamation League Task Force on Harassment and Journalism released a report in October of 2016 entitled "Anti-Semitic Targeting of Journalists During the 2016 Presidential Campaign." The report attributed just under 70% of anti-Semitic hate targeting journalists on Twitter to only 1,600 accounts. Meaning a wide majority, 1,768,000 of the 2,600,000 tweets found using keywords like "jews good old days" and "jews ovens," came from only 1,600 people, and that's assuming no one registered multiple accounts, which is charitable. The most significant spike in anti-Semitic tweets from these accounts occurred on March 13, 2016 and the following days, when Donald Trump blamed Bernie Sanders for violence at one of his rallies. Similar studies by individuals on GamerGate yielded about 2,200 accounts that appeared active for any meaningful amount of time, and about 60–70% of those tweets were retweets.

In 2017, I made a video about James Damore's Google memo, a sexist manifesto filled with biological determinism that got him fired from the company. Another YouTube user with a very right-wing audience saw it and really wanted to, I don't know, stick it to me. I guess. He made a video that repeated variants of the phrase "you didn't even read it" many times and linked to my video. He whipped his audience into a fever pitch with his characterization of me as a "deranged regressive leftist" and an "SJW male feminist" all the while making sure they remembered that link to my video. The result is over 3,500 insulting comments that contain variants of the phrase "you didn't even read it."

Whether consciously or subconsciously, that was the likely desired effect. On YouTube, many people put on a video and listen to it while they read the comments. If they did that with my video, the comments section would give the impression I didn't read it and make it seem like a waste of time. I'd bet at least a few people did legitimately not watch it due to the comments making the video seem ignorant.

I deleted all those comments and banned the users from my videos, though, because I'm not going to be branded. Make no mistake, the hope was to brand me. Unfortunately, for them, I did read it.

When *Star Wars: The Last Jedi* hit theatres later the same year, it was the second highest movie opening ever and, eventually, the fourth highest US box office total ever (behind another recent Star Wars for both). Scientific polling was conducted by several different firms (Cinemascore, ComScore, Screen Engine, etc.) in the business of predictive metrics. All three polled 90% of the audience liking it, 84% saying they'd recommend it to other people. All the firms I checked at the time predicted a $220 million opening weekend and they were all completely correct. In the meantime, the user reviews on aggregate sites like Rotten Tomatoes and Metacritic showed that about half of the reviewers hated the film and gave it 0–1 stars.

Scientific polling in the film industry involves ballots filled out by people coming out of the movie. A statistically significant number of people are polled and results are extrapolated. There is a small margin of error in scientific polling, and frankly anything can be faked, but methodology is followed (and posted on most of these firms' websites) and the people who participate *saw* the movie. User reviews require you to sign up with an email address. To check, I was able to very quickly register five Rotten Tomatoes accounts and post reviews from each. It took me about 10–15 minutes total and I affected the average five times as much as anyone polled scientifically, or at least would have if my five reviews hadn't been one, two, three, four and five stars.

I'm not saying there's nothing wrong with *The Last Jedi* or that people aren't allowed to have different taste than mine, but I am saying it was probably review bombed (both positively and negatively) by significantly less than 100,000 people. Let's be honest, 55,000 people who liked it (and 45,000 who didn't) didn't just show up on day one and leave most of the user reviews in the first few hours you could. This was a reality manipulation nerd war waged in the Marketplace of Ideas.

To reiterate, the idea market and its attention economy are not that hard to game. The way these events get covered, you'd think legitimately half the country was doing them.

But, for instance, the anti-Semitic Alt Right attack on reporters was not even as many people as GamerGate's attacks (also on reporters), which was not even one tenth of one tenth of one tenth of one tenth of one percent of the US population. Similarly, I'd love to see how many *Last Jedi* reviews came from the same IP addresses, but I doubt Rotten Tomatoes wants "easy to game" to be one of their more well-known attributes. Also, there are people still saying, "half the country voted for Trump." 18% of the total population of the United States voted for him. That's it.

As for the Alt Right, 2.6 million tweets sounds like a lot! But from only 1,600 accounts? That sounds... odd. Tiny numbers of people orchestrating what appears to be huge mobs of people who get coverage by mainstream media, as such, cloud what is really going on. When the numbers make it seem like huge amounts of people think this way, it makes the world much more frightening. The point is to make you think "maybe it's true" or "maybe they won." Because that's how you win: you seed doubt in a world that demands perfection.

But the party's over. As of today, you understand enough of this to be dangerous.

PETER COFFIN

7. PERPETUAL CORRECTNESS

It would be weird if I thought I was wrong about all this stuff. The kind of effort it has taken to write this thing has, at times, totally taken me off-guard. I'm reasonably certain I'm the only one in my family to have written a book, other than a distant relative who got shipwrecked about a century ago—and I totally get why. It is genuinely very difficult. If I had put this much of myself into something I thought was wrong, I don't know what I would think of myself—or what I would do with all the money! Pandering to people one internally disagrees with can be profitable, but just not my style. That's lazy green.

I *do* think that I am right about this. Though this is all an attempt to create framing for things that are totally abstract or metaphorical, I do believe I am not just talking out of my ass. These things have come from a lot of time, observation and reflection. It's informed by experience and study, but I also must acknowledge that this isn't scientific fact.

This is largely my opinion, but I'd like to remind you that democracy, capitalism, liberalism, conservatism and communism are largely borne from the manifestation of people's opinions, as well. What I'm saying might not end up agreeable, and it may end up not being taken seriously by academics, intellectuals, or the billions of people just living out their lives. That's fine by me. I was born in a rural area and have largely presented myself in the service of humor throughout my life. People have said a lot of frankly bizarre things about me and I exist outside the circles of "people who are normally taken seriously." I understand that.

I am fully aware that this is all coming out of *my* custom reality.

Both despite, as well as, because of this, I must think I'm right. We are all spending time trying to make sense of things in our lives that appear to be simple at the top level. But, as one becomes more knowledgeable, these things are infinitely more complex than our initial perception. I'm not the first person to raise these questions, and I'm also very likely not the first person to have had the thought that the Marketplace of Ideas is bad for collective truth because of how it plays out to commodify discourse, ideas, and other things that are not traditionally thought of as commodities. These are mechanisms for changing reality as perceived by human beings, and although I've never seen a book about all the specific things I've mentioned in relation to each other, I find it hard to believe no one has had these thoughts. Noam Chomsky and Edward Herman wrote a book in the 1980s entitled *Manufacturing Consent* that attempts to make sense of some very adjacent ideas.

Specifically asserting I'm confident in this material also acts as a case for the validity of my concepts. I think this is extremely interesting to think about; presenting the idea of the Marketplace of Ideas in the Marketplace of Ideas would likely tell you that it's valid.

Though, most assertions aren't as self-fulfilling. It takes a specific attitude to continually feel valid about much of the stuff people are screaming into cameras and microphones all over the world, and it's not "self-reflection."

When we turn on cable news, we will see any number of *experts* speaking on whatever issue is going on right now. Now, "experts" is a word and therefore subjective, but I am speaking specifically of people who have proven themselves to be *at the very least interesting*. They may possess the ability to speak on a topic or several at an acceptable level. It's *somewhat* fair to call them an expert, though not with the traditional definition of "a person who has a comprehensive knowledge or skill in a particular discipline." More appropriately, if you really wanted to point out the difference between an expert and an "expert," you could use the term "thought leader."

The function of a "thought leader" is specifically to validate everything around them. They validate the narrative, thereby validating the show, network and company they are providing commentary for. They also validate themselves, but most importantly, they validate you.

Thought leaders traffic in perpetual correctness; each one of them a televangelist for the Religion of Me, designed to ingratiate and direct demographics of people who see themselves as smart individuals making up their own minds for themselves. They carefully curate the things they want their followers exposed to, because the beauty of this system is how much agency we have. We have all agency! Smart people make choices like mine!

In the Marketplace of Ideas, thought leaders are the Salespeople of Ideas. They are, themselves, a brand that sells their perspective as a lifestyle. Sometimes they might get all humble and say "I don't have *all* the answers," but they emphasize the "all" instead of the "don't." More than anything else, though, the thought leader is getting paid. They're writing books, they're making appearances, they're doing everything someone of note might do—but there's money behind it. You see them doing native content, ads that look and read like actual articles. They might work for a think tank that acts as an intermediate between a company wishing to lobby and a politician. They might push an oil agenda but this time, it's somehow clean!

This does an amazing job integrating with our country's perception that it is operating as a meritocracy. For instance, a thought leader can most likely maintain employment. That can mean on cable news or on the assembly line, though they might not be called a "thought leader" when they are filling less visible jobs. But whether they're an author or an engineer, being perceived as an expert is an easy way for a person to reach "safe career" levels.

The hard way, obviously, is being a legitimate specialist with any degree of modesty. Not to say that building a brand and lifestyle around oneself is *easy*, but if it was easier to be a full-blown specialist, we'd probably have more of them. Possessing the ability to speak on one or more topics of interest to those who sign the checks can simply mean taking advantage of their ignorance to things like terminology, and paying attention to new developments within the sector, repeating information when convenient. Ultimately, it's just dependent on what someone will accept as an "expert."

An expert, in the context of today's media, is a necessary component in the construction of narrative. On cable news, that means an expert is either there to reinforce what the outlet wants to say, to "debunk" what someone else has said, or provide controlled opposition. Remember, the narrative needs the social capital to maintain market share and remain "valid."

Actual specialists on subjects are often on TV saying things that are provable with science, but so do the thought leaders with their cursory, TL;DR-level knowledge of the topics at hand interesting demeanor. Thought leaders fill the specialist role when a specialist can't be there (read: costs too much), doesn't exist, or wouldn't say what a producer wants a specialist to come in and say. So basically, all the time.

Eventually, thought leaders might get to host their own program. Their guests range from other thought leaders, to people who are intentionally brought in to look wrong to help the narrative in some way. Tucker Carlson, host of "Tucker Is Right And The Person In The Other Box Is Wrong And Dumb And Bad," is a thought leader. People he brings on are there to be painted as wrong.

The most important distinction to make regarding the difference between "expert" and "thought leader" is that *there aren't any distinctions made.* These roles are treated the same, regardless of whether it's a genuine specialist, a thought leader, or a schmuck setup to take a fall. A network must represent the people who fill "expert" roles *as experts.* If they didn't book experts as experts, where would they be? Certainly not in a position of credibility, that's for sure. The net effect is that everyone who gets called "expert" gets to share in the credibility of specialists, because the people who constantly have your attention *act as though they are specialists.*

Individually speaking, you may agree with them or you might say "that guy's full of shit." It's up to you, right? Regardless of what that person says, they're meant to help the narrative in some way. That can mean you think they're full of shit if it reinforces why you watch that network. Ultimately, the thing that matters is that you feel comfortable in the idea that *you* are correct.

When you have lots of people looking for competing viewpoints to reinforce their own biases and verify themselves as correct, it makes sense to pick one and give them the "best" version of what they want. Representing opposing views in a responsible, fair way might make the viewers question themselves and the information presented. Someone who is willing to do this is not an ideal viewer for a commercial break, and, therefore, bad for the bottom line. Now, it's not *just* about the bottom line; there are people involved with both better and worse motives. But if a person interested in gaining and retaining power can get a ton of people to agree with them *and* it makes them a ton of money... why wouldn't they?

We all want to be experts within our own set of standards because we all view ourselves as leaders. Whether or not we lead others isn't relevant; we're leading ourselves. Simply put, these competing narratives exist because we all follow the Religion of Me. We're all the protagonist and the savior; we all must do something extraordinary with our lives so when everyone looks back, we are recognized as the leader of the entire world!

We all must be that one guy in that one movie who kept saying the thing was going to happen, but the scientists, the government, and all the people said "no, it won't happen"—and then it happens. You know, that guy played by Jeff Goldblum. Basically, it's all a bunch of smoke and mirrors that feeds into the idea that we progress on merit.

What's the cardinal sin in a meritocracy?

If by "meritocracy," one means that power should be bestowed upon individuals based on ability or talent, then the people who excel are those with abilities and talent. The way one can explicitly show that they have abilities and talent is by being right. So, the cardinal sin is being wrong. When one is wrong, it invalidates one's entire position in a meritocracy, which we think we live in. But if we lived in a meritocracy; the "experts" would consist entirely of actual, real, *foremost* specialists. If this were a legitimate meritocracy, and your opinion is the one with merit, how would "experts" exist with views other than your own? They should only be able to get there on merit, and no doubt you believe your own philosophy and thoughts to be "of merit." So how do they have a salary?

Well, we don't live in a meritocracy, for one. We live in a world attempting to exploit us, but keep us feeling validated. So, instead, we have "thought leaders," and *you* are the judge of what's right. The net result is a personal taste that isn't just about entertainment or politics, but about *reality*.

Because your personal taste is tied so closely to the world as you see it, you must endlessly justify. This is a process that holds you dead in your tracks; you will never progress if your main activity is justification. Not to mention the fact that you must be an "expert," too. You don't have a choice; you *need* to be right. You must be equipped for conversation among your peers and superiors and you need to show that you can be relied upon.

So, what if "right" or "correct" isn't objective? What if your taste in "reality" is one that can be advocated for? Is your flavor of existence one that is profitable?

You likely can internalize information presented to you, as well as act agreeable to people in power. You might live and work in a place that is primarily "conservative" (or a place that is primarily "liberal") and you might know how to package what you say to get through to people in this environment.

Either way, you've likely heard someone say "look at all the sheeple in the Republican party, just doing everything they're told to! They're stupid!" Or you may have heard "get a load of these libtard sheeple! They just hole up in their coastal cities and don't talk to anyone who thinks differently from them!" The thread through these statements is that the opposing side is full of "followers" that need to be "herded." They essentially receive "orders" and execute them.

That's just not how you get people to do what you want them to do. People *hate* orders.

No, people aren't blind or stupid. They certainly aren't sheeple. In chapter 2, "Denial of a Collective Reality," I said everyone is encouraged to believe that the buck stops with them. We're all the protagonist of our own movie and despite our anger at others for being so self-centered, we're the customer *and the customer is always right.* In our own heads, we're Sir William Wallace, Jon Snow, Tony Stark or some other masculine hero that is foisted upon pop culture. Or, if we don't yet realize that The Matrix is a trans, anti-capitalism narrative, we're all Neo.

We're all leading ourselves. As we make our way through life, we can feel as if everyone is following *our* lead. We don't stop to check if anyone is following, we just lead like the glorious bastard we were destined to be. If we don't, then we don't even have a chance in this world. At least, that's what our supposedly merit-oriented culture is predicated on.

We're all "Leaders of None," bravely occupying spaces or making choices from drastically oversimplified information, not always presented in a binary, but most effective if done so. Republican or Democrat, conservative or liberal, Marvel or DC, Coke or Pepsi, Xbox or PlayStation, *male or female*—these choices serve to keep us in a controlled environment. They're managed choices that we feel empowered for making, because we're exercising our agency. A true leader thinks of all their people—even when the only person they're leading is themselves. As our own leaders, we rely on ourselves to make the right choice for all of me.

When presented with the opposite end of the binaries and spectrums we occupy, we become very uncomfortable. Why? Because we're always correct! We know that we picked the right side. We had to; we're the leader! When presented with something we haven't yet considered, we aren't supposed to want to consider it.

Being perceived as "correct," by both ourselves and others, validates *so much* about how this world works, including the things with which we disagree.

This can be seen in a study published in the *Psychological Bulletin* in the very last days of 2017 entitled "Perfectionism Is Increasing Over Time: A Meta-Analysis of Birth Cohort Differences From 1989 to 2016."

> *Our findings suggest that self-oriented perfectionism,*
> *socially prescribed perfectionism, and other-oriented*

perfectionism have increased over the last 27 years. We speculate that this may be because, generally, American, Canadian, and British cultures have become more individualistic, materialistic, and socially antagonistic over this period, with young people now facing more competitive environments, more unrealistic expectations, and more anxious and controlling parents than generations before.

With general social malaise as a backdrop, neoliberalism has succeeded in shifting cultural values so to now emphasize competitiveness, individualism, and irrational ideals of the perfectible self. These ideals are systemic within contemporary language patterns, the media, and social and civic institutions, and are evident in the rise of competitive and individualistic traits, materialistic behavior, and presentational anxieties among recent generations of young people.

In a meritocracy (even a fake one), being correct (even pretend correct) is power, whether that's expressing yourself in the "expert" role on television or demonstrating why you should be promoted and not another worker. When *they* are wrong by *your* standards, *you* feel powerful.

News, like any other television program, caters to demographics. So, while it may *usually* "get it right" for their audience, there is always *something* you'll say, "I'm not entirely in agreement with that" about. Ultimately, if the overall narratives validate you, then the network accomplishes what it sets out to do. They've become better over time in accomplishing this task as they have become more blatantly partisan and specific in narrative.

Algorithms do this so much more efficiently, though.

Google and Facebook aggregate and curate your experience online down to the most finite detail they can glean from the habits all those tracking cookies record. Honestly, I often feel like they named them "cookies" simply because cookies taste good and aren't related to stalking in any way. What a tasty and effective way to sound like you're not stalking people!

Instead of television producers, there's probabilities based on your previous habits. Computers are faster than a human being, and it doesn't matter if they're right or not; they're presenting you what you choose from. When you see something on these services, it's because the algorithm deems it "best for you," or relevant to your interests. Considering what is required of a person in their everyday lives, somewhere in your interests is "being right."

Being right is extremely comforting. That comfort itself is so specific that I'd call it a particular type of comfort, as well. It's special because, in the traditional sense, one could be extremely uncomfortable—even in danger—and if one was correct that it was going to happen or about how it would happen, somewhere inside we'd be saying, "I knew it." Despite whatever terrible thing is happening, we are at least validated in that way.

9/11 produced an entire industry of people who were Perpetually Correct™. They were right about who was the problem, what they were going to do next, and what we should do about it. Obviously, this turned out really well. The result was definitely not that; by estimates in peer-reviewed research from a 2013 report published in *PLOS Medicine* entitled "Mortality in Iraq Associated with the 2003–2011 War and Occupation" arrived at, a half million private citizens in Iraq were killed in a war that Wasn't About Oil™. Clearly, that wasn't the outcome.

NARRATOR: "That *was* the outcome."

On every level, the post-9/11 machine incentivized speculation on a massive level and resulted in what is arguably genocide. It was inarguably imperialistic and in the service of a few profiteers, and yet people bent over backwards to justify their own support for "spreading democracy." People who were in the government, the media, and every walk of private citizen were bending over backwards to go scorch Iraq again. A series of societal biases, combined with the context of a decade of war that painted Saddam Hussein as "Hitler: The Sequel" and then questionable links to 9/11, made it make sense to want to go to war in Iraq again. Nary an oil baron or a private military contractor had an argument against it, either.

In fact, questioning going into Iraq was viewed as heretical. While some might paint that as groupthink, I would like to propose something different: tons of "experts" and everyday people who all considered themselves the primary authority on everything were all saying something similar, so everyone said "look at all these people telling me I'm right! Everyone agrees with me!" Everyone was the protagonist at a time when protagonists who supported the Iraq War played well with audiences.

Do you remember what it was like back in 2003 to say, "maybe we shouldn't invade Iraq?" It was basically like saying "women don't like nice guys" *nowadays*, except for the fact that we *actually shouldn't have invaded Iraq*. But that wasn't "correct." Unless you said it to *some* folks on the left, then it was.

Neither Twitter nor Facebook were around back then, but can you picture the discourse on either leading up to an Iraq invasion? I can only imagine how sky high all the metrics would have been when arguments were running hot in that era. Regardless of what anyone posted, it would have received a lot of engagement, which feels *great*. It's proof you're right—not just to you, but to the algorithms, too.

The more detailed a profile on how to make you feel right, the more specific the advertisements that get shown to you. The advertisements show you positive versions of things in which the algorithm believes you'd be interested. Then maybe you'll talk about it if you check it out. If you're a "thought leader," you *will*—and you will try to be first. Oh, and here's the kicker: we're all meant to think we're thought leaders and we're all first in our own lives. We all did everything before it was cool and everyone else is behind the times.

When you feel the comfort of perpetual correctness, you're more likely to be receptive towards ad messages, because they're only presenting positive information for you to decide with, and you don't feel the need to ask other people for input—why would you? What you think is true. You are "right."

There's an element of self-preservation, as well. The perpetually correct are more likely to point at a symptom of a problem *as the problem* and say: "That's bad. See this? It's bad. So bad. How bad, bad, bad, BAD!" However, if the system that created that problem comes up, there's nothing to be said.

When I say, "Logan Paul," what do you think? Japan Suicide Forest, right? How much discourse surrounding that event had anything to do with systemic racism? Almost none. Everything was about how bad every person thinks Logan Paul is. True, I wouldn't mind pouring laxative into his warm 2% milk or whatever he drinks before bed. But a conversation could have easily been had about racism that isn't outwardly malicious, but because it's racism, it still has that net effect of maliciousness. We're talking about the kind of racism where people have no idea they are racist.

Or hey, instead of telling people to retweet if you care about suicide victims, maybe let's talk about something related to suicide. Yeah, it's good to get suicide prevention phone numbers out there, but what about people who are constantly haunted by thoughts of suicide. Why did it need to wait until Logan Paul did something ignorant and vaguely racist? Why is there so much stigma in discussing suicide? What is it that causes suicide? Is it the fact mental health is neglected in our health system? Is it that our health system is for-profit, that it makes more sense not to indulge in maintenance care, the kind that most mental health care is? Is it that emergencies are significantly more profitable, not only because of their high dollar amounts, but also because insurance companies are more likely to pay out those high dollar amounts?

In my frankly lazy analysis here, I've now talked more about systems than everyone did when that whole thing blew up. However, addressing that would end the perpetuity of one's correctness, because the problem could be solved due to the mass acknowledgement and demand for a solution. Twitter is absolutely wonderful for this, because there's this loop where you just pick a thing that is obviously bad, call it bad, and accept the sweet, sweet spike in metrics without any thought deeper than surface-level.

Thought leaders have a vested interest in criticizing symptoms, because they need something to be right about. Everyone participating in this system needs to be right, including the people who own everything, the people who appear on cable news, and yourself.

So, is the media totally worthless? You may be surprised to hear me say this, but absolutely not. Indeed, there are a plethora of issues based in this profit-driven perspective-as-fact popularized by Fox News but employed by basically any news outlet which has profit at its heart.

There are situations where the media can be worse; I pointed to "alternative facts" because it's an obvious issue, but "alternative" media can be just as bad as (if not, much worse than) mainstream media. Then there's state-owned media, which has legitimately no incentive whatsoever to question any authority the government amasses. There are many obvious problems that can arise from that, as well. The situation we have is, amazingly, not the worst it could be. However, most agree that we are closer to "the worst" than we should be, at least if you don't ask them any partisan questions.

However, just "not being the worst it can be" is not a good reason to avoid discussing it.

The Religion of Me, individualism, is not a functional societal philosophy. We have information and entertainment reinforcing it at every turn, validating our every assertion before we even have the time to reflect on them ourselves. This is not to say we must invalidate the individual, just that we need to stop centering society so completely on the concept of the perfect, rationally acting individual.

To go a step further, things like gender identity and expression are not threats to collective reality. These are issues that one attends to on a personal level and, regardless of how one chooses to proceed, do not actually impact other people in a negative way. Agency and diversity are important ideals—ones I advocate for. On top of that, there's peer-reviewed behavioral and biological science that backs a lot of people's assertions up, with new research happening all the time. Standardized information can be checked; experiments can be repeated. If the results replicate, there's reason to believe something may be collectively true.

There is an inherent issue with scientific studies, though: they're often behind a paywall. Research costs money, which has to come from somewhere. This is one of many reasons information scientific methodology yields get shielded from public view. Besides that, withholding information is vital to controlling people who retain agency, so outlets that disagree with the information are likely not to disseminate it.

Keeping everyone feeling as if they are correct is a balancing act. It's incredibly fragile and necessitates a singular, predominant mode of operation in which no one *solves* anything. If you can represent yourself as an expert on how things are *right now,* then this is the situation in which you can profit—that means everyday people in normal jobs and every single person up the hierarchy. We are specifically comfortable when we are correct because being correct seems to lead us to a more generally comfortable existence. Just *feeling* correct might not yield that same result, but Pavlov proved the result isn't necessary to reinforce the behavior. Just the promise.

Ultimately, The American Dream is that promise. Do you still believe in it?

PETER COFFIN

8. CULTIVATED IDENTITY

"Who am I?" We ask ourselves this question all the time. We ask it at important crossroads, in times of need, and with our head on the pillow after even the most uneventful of days. It is the most basic human question of all and the answer can elude even the best of us.

One of the most interestingly worded definitions for "identity" I've seen is "the characteristics of determining one's fact of being." I find it interesting for a couple of reasons. The first is that, of course, "fact" is not objective; this definition makes it even more apparent. The second is that those who argue *against* the idea a person can be marginalized by their identity often say, "it's fact." You hear it all the time: "there's only two genders; that's fact" or "there's just more crime in black communities; that's fact." Some folks will ignore all the research, deny that context influences the effect statistics have, and otherwise choose not to believe peer-reviewed evidence.

It's interesting that the people who argue that "fact is universal" or that something can be "objectively true" are usually the ones who ignore the use of scientific methodology (or other collective methodology) to further our societal understanding of things. Demanding a human-created idea be considered universal is a ridiculous overstatement of humanity's importance in the universe. Yeah, *we're* objective. Us.

It might sound like I'm saying humanity has a superiority complex, but I think it's quite the opposite. There is very little which reveals fragility more conspicuously than demanding one's assertions be considered universal. The fragile often want to appear infallible, but in loudly asserting they are the latter often look the former. To be human is mandatorily inclusive of weakness; to deny weakness is to deny humanity.

Why would someone so desperately want to deny that which makes them human?

Perpetual correctness explains some of it; in a perceived meritocracy you must be right *or else*. There is only one path to comfort and that's continually looking as though you are intellectually superior to the people around you. Being confronted with being wrong impedes our path to being perceived as being an expert. Someone who is wrong by their target demographic's standards *even sometimes* can hardly be perceived as a thought leader.

Talking about merit and perpetual correctness is talking about external pressures and socialization, though. These expectations "inspire" many to aspire to be the next Steve Jobs, and so many will consider themselves failures for never having met those expectations. Still, that is an exchange with society rather than an internal one; thought leadership is a means to produce or profit. But how does one consume?

To find and understand the processes behind that, we only have to look at fandom.

"Fan" is a late 19th century abbreviation for "fanatic." A fanatic is "a person filled with excessive and single-minded zeal, especially for an extreme religious or political cause." Basically, an obsessive person whose interest and enthusiasm for something is extreme. In more recent parlance, people say "fan" more casually in place of simply saying "enjoyer of." Most who say "fan" do not mean "obsessive," and I am not asserting that it automatically means that. Yet, you do see quite a few people who specifically identify as a fan of something often tend to be just that.

Someone who identified as a Limp Bizkit fan in the 1990s often dressed like the band's frontman, Fred Durst. They'd have on a backwards red, fitted baseball cap, a white t-shirt with the band logo, and khakis. Someone who liked Metallica in the 1980s probably wore faded jeans and a black t-shirt with the band logo. People who supported Hillary Clinton in 2016, are now carrying around a copy of *What Happened* and wearing a blue t-shirt with that bad "H" logo (with the arrow pointing *right* for whatever reason).

She may have charted better if she had toured more in support of her album...

Being a fan of someone or something means more than you might think. It doesn't matter if we're talking about Star Wars or the Republican Party. I mention both because I want you to understand this isn't about anything specific. Everything has "fandom," no matter what it is. This applies to entertainment, a political party, a religion, an activity, and everything you can consume.

It's important to understand that I'm very specifically not talking about *just liking something*. What I mean to highlight and criticize is the phenomenon of capital interests pushing people to incorporate enjoyment of a thing one likes into one's identity. This is intended to continue in an ever-increasing capacity with the intention of extracting more and more value through consumption.

It could be popular culture, or it could be a deeply held belief that becomes obsession and overrides the people and activities that make up their lives. When a person's identity is on the line, criticism of one's treasured thing starts to feel extremely important. I also believe that all of us acquiesce to at least some degree of this aspect of socialization in capitalism. However, I very much want people to understand I am not saying that enjoyment of things is bad or that responsibility for this rests on any individual. It is not you who is cultivating your identity; it is capital that is extracting value from you. Think of it like a crop on a factory farm; the farmer plants seed, nurtures and harvests.

By cultivating identity, marketing can encourage a person to act as if they own a thing they love, despite not being involved in the process of creating it. The perspective capital often wishes to cultivate is that *the fan* gives the words meaning. This is mildly similar to "death of the author," if the concept were more about ownership than interpretation. In the fan's mind, *they* own this thing someone else has worked on.

This is actually not an outlandish reaction, if you think about it. Fans have purchased the object of their enjoyment, either directly or via related merchandise. Not only do they literally purchase media and merchandise, they metaphorically "buy it," as well. The purchase occurred both physically and in the Marketplace of Ideas. Fans give the brand their attention, which in a world where everything is commodified and framed as a market, is an investment. One might call it an emotional one.

In defense of this thing, or rather, *the fan's investment in the thing*, they can bother, troll, trick, threaten, harass, stalk and even abuse. This is a bit like being correct and obtaining or retaining merit, but not entirely. When a fan has reached this point, criticism becomes a perceived threat to their very identity, which often evokes an emotional response.

Regarding "attentionomics," expression of emotion is often regarded as attention-seeking. As said earlier, this is analogous to profit-seeking. Fandom is a place where one is given the justification to express emotion, because it is done in a manner that feeds into the actual profit-seeking of whatever company owns the rights to the thing people like. This legitimizes this kind of attention-seeking in the eyes of fans; it contributes to a thing they derive identity from, rather than specifically for themselves. This can be taken as "contributing to the community," and therefore excuses the emotional outbursts that fans might criticize *in others* as "irrational."

The positive effect of surrendering one's identity to capital are new places to belong: castles, pirate ships, or beyond the stars. A fan might label where they come to belong as a "community," but it's not as simple as that. Community has several definitions. There's "a group of people living in the same area," but this is obviously not relevant as fandom is often spread around many locales and connected over the internet. The definitions that matter in this conversation are "fellowship with others, due to sharing common attitudes, interests and goals" as well as "a group with similarity of identity." Given the identity we are talking about is one cultivated by and for the interests of capital, fandom can act and feel very much like community. However, I would assert that at its core, it is more a validation gang. Which might hurt, because you are probably a fan of something. If so, it is not me who is hurting you.

"Toxic fandom" is something we likely all carry a degree of, even if the subject of our admiration is overtly progressive. The reason? Marketing doesn't ask us to consume in a healthy way. In fact, the goal is that we will consume as much as possible, which depending on the tactics used, can easily exploit the vulnerable or naive. Most people are (at the very least) naive to the way marketing works; more research than you can imagine has been put into creating effective marketing.

A man you may not have heard of is Edward Bernays. He was born November 22nd, 1891, and lived 103 years. He was Sigmund Freud's nephew. I'm not dealing with Freud in this book—he did contribute some useful things but a larger amount of the opposite.

Freud was Freud, but his ideas did lead Bernays to create highly effective marketing theory. Bernays was an artist when it came to creating material and circumstances that caused outcomes he desired. Though he did start specifically in the realm of marketing, he wrote the book on propaganda. I am not using that as a figure of speech. He wrote a book entitled *Propaganda* that is essentially "how to propaganda."

What you may find interesting is that the book functions as propaganda *for propaganda*. He not only lays out his theories, but he does everything to normalize and popularize propaganda as a method for maintaining an elite, as much as it encourages consumption. Step one, do *not* call it propaganda. Call the stuff that the bad guys do, propaganda. *We do public relations here.*

Among his ideas was attaching a product to a person's self-image and their expression of it, tapping into their desires and preferences, or what you and I today might call identity. Materials he wrote told people outright to express themselves through performative consumption. Here's what he had a spokesperson for one of his campaigns say:

> *There's a psychology of dress. Have you ever thought about it, how it can express your character? You all have interesting characters, but some of them are all hidden. I wonder why you all want to dress always the same. With the same hats and the same coats. I'm sure all of you are interesting and have wonderful things about you. But looking at you in the street, you all look so much the same. And that's why I'm talking to you about the psychology of dress. Try and express yourselves better in your dress.*

He's arguably the originator of this. Over the following decades, other theorists tinkering with and building on his ideas came up with a framework we now know as lifestyle marketing.

This, despite Bernays not personally believing a damn word of it. Where you might find the theorists who created "Values and Lifestyles," the basic methodological scaffolding that lifestyle marking is built on, are true believers, Bernays wanted to use it in aid of the creation of a controllable population.

As it turns out, he vehemently agreed with some of Freud's other ideas. The one he leaned hardest into was the idea that all people hold depraved desires that need redirection or they would certainly carry them out. This led Bernays to believe that the theories he created should be used to control the populace. When dominance is the goal, actual validity in theory is much less important than creativity and drive.

In so many words, we're asked to pledge fealty and opt-in to a sub-economy based entirely around a thing we might like. We enter a reality in which there's a version of everything just for us. There is chopped lettuce branded with Star Wars and I am not joking.

The level of commitment we would need to feel excited about branded lettuce with Rey on the bag is vast, so criticism would feel dire. No, I'm not saying Star Wars fans all have to be careful about their bowels when they see a Star Wars brand chopped lettuce. I *am* saying that Disney would consider it ideal if Star Wars fans all were shitting their pants for Star Wars lettuce. Well, at least if the movements were caused by excitement and not E. coli.

It feels like an attack on our fandom and, therefore, our identity. We own enough merchandise or have consumed enough information to show that we shouldn't be questioned. For this, we're awarded the designation of "real fan." We take on this status in situations where we don't even realize we are fans, too. Certainly, Donald Trump has a fandom, and some of them likely consider themselves "the real deal" for having more of those shitty hats than someone else, or for having been to more rallies. They're "real fans," damn it!

Such a title is an illusion, though. It's only meant to create an aspirational level of fandom to exclude people and contribute to the alienation one can experience—to create feelings of longing. One could say it is easier to get people to long for something that isn't real; they can never have Crash Bandicoot go on a date with them or whatever.

Some kids don't get *all* the toys. In schoolyard conversation, it may come out that they don't have *all the toys*, leaving them open to the question of whether they actually like the thing. The words "real fan" get used, establishing a consumption-driven hierarchy. Nothing would make a kid feel better than to just have that stuff— to be a "real fan." Having more toys means the child has indisputably proven they meant it when they said, "I like this." They are a peer or even a superior, rather than a wannabe. Simply being born to parents whose situation allows for the purchase of more toys makes them "real fans."

The next stop on this ride is ownership, where "real fans" dictate what happens with something. They know better than the creators, the "lesser" fans, and (especially) anyone with criticism.

The tricky part is, buying merchandise isn't evil. None of us are wasteful monsters who are ruining something for others when we buy this stuff; we are people and shouldn't be told how to like things. We are not deliberately supporting corporate greed, and that's not automatically a conduit to acting abusively on the internet.

I'd even go so far as to say that the problem with this kind of co-opted, profit-driven identity is that it's built on top of things that are basically good. To cultivate this kind of identity, capital takes advantage of something normal and healthy: our enjoyment of cool shit. Just like individualism, the construct doesn't trick anyone, nor does anyone need to "fall for it." It's a series of many tiny pushes in a direction one *already wants to go in*, albeit with the intention of pushing one further than they originally wanted to go.

Somewhere in there, our enjoyment of something stops being just enjoyment. I believe there is a slow transformation that happens as pieces of us are linked with pieces of the thing that's being advertised. Marketers find new ways to make the little things in our life remind us of their products, services and lifestyles. They also work to remind you there's someone (or a group) out there trying to stop you from enjoying what you like. The intent is to nurture dependence that mutates into something with elements of fixation, ownership, control, fragility and (most of all) identity.

To explain with a pop culture reference: Stephen King's *Misery*.

Gamers, the "alt right," white feminists, anti-vaxxers, militant Vegans™, "carnetarians" and Star Wars Fans are all groups you might applaud or cringe at the mention of. This is mostly due to these groups' propensity to be exclusive. But what do they all have in common? Is there a shared trait between these seemingly unrelated groups? What exactly are these things?

If you're buying what capital is selling, they are identities.

What I'm describing is typically referred to as "consumer identity" and "consumer culture," but I would argue the inclusion of the word "consumer" is too positive sounding. The term sounds as though it's positive, perhaps even a recognition of the customer's individuality and culture. That's not what it is.

Consumer culture is a carefully curated set of social norms with an agenda—profit. It's easier to profit (either monetarily or socially) when people identify with a controlled, predictable culture where the only real choice is assimilation.

This is why I feel that a better term for "consumer identity" is "cultivated identity."

Cultivation of identity, as previously stated, is an act performed by capital. It is the subconscious defining of people's essence in a manner that suits an intended purpose. This is enacted by putting a "consumable" at (or near) the center of a person's identity. One might think by "consumable" I mean a physical product that can be purchased with fiat currency. I intend to instill a wider definition of "consumable," however. Here, when I say "consumable," I mean everything from a product, a TV show, a franchise, a point of view or a person. I derive the concept of consumption and hyperconsumption from the work of a writer by the name of Trudy, whose brilliant writings start at a blog she ran called Gradient Lair and *do not stop*. If you have time and the inclination to read more material that my work here derives insight from (and a wealth of other insight), I highly recommend her work.

It's essentially impossible for an identity forming around a consumable to have a fully formed set of ideals, but it does have tenets and requirements of its own. The associated lifestyle marketing will continually push a person to concentrate more on the consumable (simply by associating feelings with it rather than further discussion of it) and eventually can put one's identity in a very fragile position.

Commercials and other brand messaging might sell consumers on adventure, a look, a feeling, the good ol' days, the future, caring, not caring or *whatever*. A company puts its logo on all this content, but concentrates on associating the brand with the experience they attempt to curate. Lifestyle marketers invest a great deal of time and money into content to which they believe consumers will relate. The intent is to create managed culture and identity, rather than to claim their product as the best.

Even so, people need to be primed to consume or it's all for naught.

PETER COFFIN

9. PRO-CONSUMER OR PRO-CONSUMPTION

To be "pro-consumer" sounds like a really good thing. One wouldn't be a fool to take it to mean "advocacy on behalf of the consumer," meaning the end user of a product, service, or other consumable. This sounds like a noble endeavor. The consumer is but an individual, and their power pales in comparison to that of a corporation; what a truly wonderful thing to stand up for them. However, I believe the terms "pro-consumer" and "pro-consumption" are often confused.

Amazon brands itself as very "pro-consumer," but a lot of its "pro-consumer" activities don't have the objective of increasing accountability on their end, but rather simply encourage more consumption. They "make it easier" to order with the Buy Now With 1-Click® button, which reduces the number of steps needed to purchase something. They also have a priority shipping service that makes individual purchases seem cheaper and faster. They even have physical buttons one can connect to WiFi to press when one runs out of something. That's right! You can buy buttons that you press to buy other products.

The only way this is "pro-consumer" is that they are actively pursuing *the state of having consumers*. They are not protecting the "consumer" from exploitation engaged in by an entity with significantly more power than the average individual, *like themselves*. Instead, Amazon is simply streamlining the purchase process, removing points where a customer might say "actually I'm not going to buy it." More transactions are becoming impulse buys as we have less time to slow down and consider what we're doing.

Consumers are being given easier paths to consume, and therefore their lives are being made easier. Consumption is genuinely a large part of life, whether it is the primary means to enforce hierarchy or isn't. We must consume food and water whether we're "consumers" or not, it's just that, at some point, someone figured out that controlling food and water meant controlling people.

Nobody wants to be just "a consumer," though. Consumption isn't an identity. Don't believe me? Ask someone "is consumption identity?" and very few, if any, people would answer with "oh yeah, I am a sum of the things I consume and nothing more!"

Yet, we don't just play video games; we *are* "gamers." We're not eating a vegan diet; we're Vegans™.

We all have our own brands, hierarchies, validation gangs, thought leaders, and our own perception of what is correct. At the center of all of it is us, the reluctantly smart protagonist of our own film, making all the right decisions. Whatever we consume, we're right about it. Whatever we say, we're right about it. People may not believe us, but that is at their own peril. We knew the aliens were coming. We knew Facebook was Black Mirror. Just us, just me, and just you. All of us, individually, are the only ones that know anything.

We're not naturally so self-absorbed, though; the world is simply made to seem focused on us. We are merely responding in kind.

Paul Mazur, a prominent figure at Lehman Brothers from 1923 until his retirement in 1977, was a primarily financier for consumer goods firms. In 1927, Mazur said the following in a piece he wrote for the Harvard Business Review:

> *We must shift America, from a needs to a desires culture. People must be trained to desire, to want new things even before the old have been entirely consumed. We must shape a new mentality in America. Man's desires must overshadow his needs.*

Paul Mazur was not alone in this sentiment; his contemporaries said similar things in other articles a and essays. Mazur is more significant because he ended up a consultant on the "New Deal," which should contextualize that effort a bit. Yes, a lot of business people fought tooth-and-nail against anything that could possibly limit them in any way. But people with a better understanding of where America was headed and how to use it thought it made sense that consumers not only wanted to consume, but could, would, and (most importantly) wouldn't stop.

These things get so embedded in who we are that they eventually become our defining traits. Many of us take "who are you," to mean "what consumption do you want to be associated with?" We would never admit it, especially to ourselves, but how many times has "fan" passed your lips when asked to describe yourself? Did you feel vindicated when I talked about the fact The Last Jedi user reviews were likely gamed? Does it feel good seeing someone bolster something you enjoyed consuming? Or were you one of the people that gamed them?

You rat bastard.

Validity of art in the "nerd" realm, be it videogames, comics, or blockbuster movies, is framed almost entirely from a business perspective. There are conventions, announcements, metrics, metascores, rankings, revenue reports... Other than the works of art themselves, essentially all the talk surrounding them is overtly commerce-oriented. This talk is not, by any stretch, about how best to ensure consumers are treated well, either. It's about how well multinational corporations are doing.

How well did this game that I love sell? What was the metacritic score? How was this film's Rotten Tomatoes percentage... not the critic one, the user one? That's accurate, right? What was the box office? More people agreeing with us means we were right, and the more right we are the better position we are in to be comfortable in whatever hierarchy we take part in. Therefore, people with no financial or artistic stake take entertainment so seriously; from their perspective, this is about their place in societal hierarchy. Their taste is Certified Fresh™.

It's not pro-consumer talk. It's pro-consumption talk. "Pro-consumer" means regulations, consumer protections, and transparency. "Pro-consumption" means "feed me my fandom shit just how I like it, bitch."

So, what are consumer protections? I'll quote Wikipedia because the volunteers there put it very plainly:

Consumer protection is a group of laws and organizations designed to ensure the rights of consumers as well as fair trade, competition and accurate information in the marketplace.

Essentially, consumer protections are regulations on the market and watchdogs ensuring they're followed. This means if one were genuinely "pro-consumer," they would be least partially against the "Free Market." Keep in that in a market situation, freedom doesn't mean "the state of being unhindered in thought and expression," but rather a complete lack of regulations. This ensures that trade will not be fair, because fair means different things to different people. To a profiteer, it is fair to swindle a person because they "should have known better." Combining that with all I've said so far in this book (environmental control, perpetual correctness, cultivated identity, the marketplace of ideas, etc.) it sounds like a loaded deck, which obviously isn't fair. Clearly consumer protections are meant to change that; you can even see it in the definition, plain as day: "fair trade."

The Fair-Trade movement demands regulation and accountability in working conditions and other aspects of trade. But the very idea of regulation is against "Free" Trade. That's not to say the Fair Trade movement has it 100% right; there's still a great deal of exploitation that goes on even within the parameters they set forth. Anyone who pretends Whole Foods isn't exploitative knows just how to get a laugh out of me.

The point is, "consumers" are viewed simply as a resource by those looking to extract value from them. Consumers are to be cultivated, not protected. They're harmed by addiction-encouraging business practices and the only way to make that seem normal is through the creation of "culture" that ties their identities to their unending consumption and sidestepping the idea of this consumption being a possible problem. Instead, it's proof you're a "real fan." You're a "true believer" a "legit supporter," or "an actual Democrat." When this happens successfully, they convert someone into a "hyperconsumer."

This is largely why the gaming world complains a lot about microtransactions, but tolerates them. If there hyperconsumers among them were to bite the hand that feeds, their One True Emotional Outlet™, other people might see the thing they derive identity from as "weak" because Real Fans™ attack it. It's also why when they do attack, it's out of perceived ownership and a belief that the fan just knows better. But no one outside video games cares about the "strength" of gaming; it's profitable and it isn't going away anytime soon. Similarly, Vegans™ aren't suddenly not going to have meatless food. There's no *real* danger, but a company still benefits greatly from more obsessive advocates.

This model works extremely well and that is *terrifying* to me. It's continues to leak into every aspect of our lives, too. Notice how it costs $5.99 to watch a movie on a plane now, bougies? It used to be free! Bottled water is a microtransaction, one that's older than gaming. Anyone who is pro-consumer would care about that *significantly more* than if Some Localized Video Game™ had the best boobies and booby physics it can have.

Before you ask: yes, that is something "gamers" consider "pro-consumer."

As I mentioned earlier, the cultivation of identity often includes an element of demagoguery; to point at foes (real or imaginary) that threaten the thing you like. A superhero franchise, titty anime, video games, a political party, or a space opera absolutely cannot occupy a healthy person's life entirely, so there must be threats to it. Everything that contradicts the consumable, even slightly, is labeled one of these threats, and it *really* doesn't matter if the contradiction is only a perceived one. For instance, "western censorship" isn't a real threat to titty anime as long as oversized cartoon breasts make some company in Japan money.

These threats are to be addressed by various means - and various statistics (sales figures, metacritic scores) or acknowledgements (GOTY, Grammys, or even just good reviews) are seen as justification for whatever action is taken. "Would it have gotten that attention if we hadn't made a stink?"

Often, there is subtle implication that if that threat were not there, everything would be better, but eventually the thing may win the approval of the "threatening" group. This is called "crossover success" and is how something becomes mainstream. Lots of it.

If the market gets to the point of needing to include the people in the group previously considered a threat, though, a company will likely begin to cater to them. For the company, there is no need to view them as a threat anymore, because they'll happily buy the lifestyle and products associated with it. This makes the company SELL OUTS. In encouraging Hyperconsumption, companies nurture people down a path where they can easily turn on those cultivating their identities. In fact, is say it's inevitable if something becomes successful in the mainstream. If the thing they derive identity from suddenly contradicts that identity, everything goes haywire.

This is what GamerGate was: a perceived "threat to gaming as-is" in the form of increased participation from women (considered members of an out-group) and a wider variety of core tenants. The industry that previously labeled these people and things as threats seemingly embracing these changes. Star Wars fans did the same. Three times now: "a female lead!? A black stormtrooper!? POC!? REBUTTAL OF CAPITALISM AND THE MILITARY INDUSTRIAL COMPLEX!? SJW INVASION!"

Ultimately, this is all interfering with their perfect experience, as promised by an entity in exchange for a pledge to consume. Pop culture and fandom is an easy place to point out identity cultivated by capital and why they do it. As I've said, though, it's embedded in everything, including politics.

Before continuing, let's clarify that "identity politics" is not directly related to what we're calling cultivated identity here. Identity as a category of political concern can be extremely important as representation of various non-consumer cultures and identities. It's tantamount to a legitimate democracy (the Civil Rights Movement was a direct result of black identity politics). An organic identity, one not cultivated by profit-seekers, has environmental and situational traits that create different perspective that is sorely needed in politics. Organic identity legitimately informs opinions and cultivated identity exists to influence opinions.

That isn't to say identity can't be co-opted to become cultivated. Nor do I wish to imply that the identity of any percentage of people is 100% cultivated or 100% organic; this is most likely not true. I simply wish to draw the distinction that "identity politics" is a totally different thing.

Flavia Dzodan, a writer who deserves much more credit than she gets, was the person who coined the phrase "my feminism will be intersectional or it will be bullshit." What is non-commodified, intersectional feminism if not a cross-section of identity and class as categories of political concern? Kimberlé Crenshaw, the originator of intersectionality, engaged in deep critical analysis to create the idea. These things aren't marketing; they're deconstruction of marketing. That's not to say no one has ever or will ever attempt to co-opt them. It is to say *we are not talking about the political concern of identity*, a point I want to make abundantly clear before the next piece of criticism.

That now said, I want to point to Hillary Clinton's "#ImWithHer" messaging as a blatant attempt at cultivating identity. In three words, it does the work of totally absolving the politician for which it supports from direct responsibility or transparency and encourages the creation of a validation gang.

"I'm" is very direct. It's immediately asking *you* to declare this is about you and who you are.

"With" functionally bonds "I'm" to whatever comes next: it essentially works as the pledge. If you accept the messaging, your allegiance lies to the final word...

"Her." Not ideas, a platform, or ideals, you're with a person. Whatever this person says or does, that is what "I'm with."

You are to validate that person and they are to validate you. That is the contract. This demands flexibility on the part of both parties, but it also demands allegiance from everyone who is not Hillary Clinton. Her marketing team, like every other marketing team ever, wants to avoid scrutiny.

If one's identity depends on something being as one perceives it to be, whoever benefits will not likely to want anyone to critically analyze it. Knowing that an identity derived from a consumable is a fragile one, if one were to find inconsistencies in the thing one derives identity from, that identity then comes into question. Public figures and politicians intentionally make themselves and their messaging into consumables, and Hillary Clinton is not exceptional.

Nor is Donald Trump. He engages in this very same insidious manipulation of his following, but with a much better handle on how to do it. Where "I'm With Her" is obvious cultivation of identity, Donald Trump can accomplish it by performance of things you would take for granted. That's not to say he legitimately understands all of this; I believe it just comes naturally to him.

Regardless of intent, what do you think happens when Donald Trump got people to raise their right arm and pledge their vote to him during the campaign, though? Do you think that he thinks it's just a fun thing to do? Do you think he *really* wants people to think he's Hitler? No. It's probably simpler than that; he wants people to think about when they pledged to the flag as a child. He wants to trigger the emotion of being a "true" American. The kind that openly, proudly says "I pledge allegiance!" He wants to open his huge yap and eat those feelings the same way I eat at a good All-You-Can-Eat Chinese buffet.

You might think I'm taking this a bit too seriously, but I'd say not. Your subconscious takes it as seriously as I do. But more importantly, marketers take it significantly more seriously.

A subset of hyperconsumers that will reliably purchase and advocate the consumable from an uncritical viewpoint is the most valuable thing a marketer could ask for: a perpetual motion machine. Forget the idea of being pro-consumer; become a Pro Consumer™.

There's consumptive behavior in almost all modern identities, whether organic or cultivated. The issue is not consumption; an individual has no choice but to consume "needs" and life without consuming some "wants" as well... sucks. The issue is that this is a system that has made consumption into more than just "eating" or "watching" in attempts to make business models that function predictably. Identity that is created by marketing quickly morphs into to incentivizing consumption with perceived friendship, community, and a feeling of validation. Strong incentive can lead only to hyperconsumption in those most receptive, which can be really frightening, aggressive behavior.

Simply addressing that behavior doesn't address their fragile identity, though. Because that doesn't get addressed, people will constantly feel as if they are under attack because different things they identify with are all tied to competing corporate and social interests.

One of the worst, most ingrained cultivated identities is "MAN" (yes, in all caps). The consumable in this case is "literally everything, except with stainless steel and black rubber."

So much of what is out there for people to consume is branded in a way that MEN will find it palatable, therefore unobjectionable to like in the presence of other MEN. This is the ultimate form of avoiding critique, in my opinion. Look at the abuse masculinity has brought the world. Hell, look at the abuse masculinity has brought to the people who consider themselves MEN.

Because everything is framed through marketplace scenarios, because we are all competing for attention in The Marketplace of Ideas, we all want to find something that makes us superior to others. If we can't do it through "thought leadership," we can as "the best consumer."

In our current system, ownership of a creative work is something one would supposedly know to ascribe to the creator of that work. The dynamic is sometimes looked at as parental, with the artist giving birth to art. In market-driven, neoliberal society, it's looked a intellectual property, which generally regards ownership a broadcast rather than a conversation. This makes it something is owned by an entity and distributed like food. Consumption does not create ownership.

On paper, we "know" the creator is "the owner" of the work because that is what we are raised to believe. It's only "fair," after all. It's interesting, though, that in the age of lifestyle marketing this is how we ideologically view creative work. Why, you ask? Well, because in practice, we don't think that way.

Today, consuming something also means buying accessories, like buying t-shirts that tell other people you like that product (and if they like it too, you're potential "friends"). Also, we're subscribing to the official monthly crate for that brand (only $24 a month). Finally, where would we be if we didn't click like on that product's Facebook page, so their algorithm knows to show you whatever other ridiculous products it decides to be related to "titty anime." That's what you clicked like on, right? Don't lie, your feed is public.

We allow this consumptive situation because we live in a cultural environment that is not complete. Today's world often withholds the opportunity to experience substance, instead offering a shallow, marketable version of every place, thing, idea, or whatever. Guy Debord talked about this in his 1967 book "The Society of The Spectacle."

Debord asserted that modern society essentially does not have an authentic social life. Instead, it's co-opted by representation and performance. He outlines a process by which a phenomenon he calls "Spectacle" takes effect as "the decline of being into having, and having into merely appearing." He said that getting to this point is regarded as the "moment at which the commodity completes its colonization of social life." One could say that the

fe we've discussed in this book is just

at "passive identification with the
genuine activity," which is so damn
saying, it should bother you. "The
llection of images. Rather, it is a social
n people that is mediated by images."
Debord essentially predicted HGTV and TLC.

"Organic" identity is developed by an environment that
informs our views, by other people we know and love, and
by the individual's interpretation of these things. It's not
automatically good, either. Cultivated identity is the result
of an inauthentic environment tailored to encourage
consumption by means of tying it to one's identity. I
alluded to it earlier, but I think we all exist at some point
on a spectrum between these two things. I very much
doubt it's possible, at least in current conditions, to have an
entirely organic or an entirely cultivated identity.

Sometimes one might observe a disconnect: there is
identity obviously cultivated by capital and there is also
identity that *acts as if it was but wasn't.* A lot of people act as
if their identity has been cultivated by capital even if it
hasn't been directly.

A good example of this would be that whole "Rick and
Morty" Szechuan Sauce debacle. The TV show made a
joke about one of the main characters being totally
obsessed with a sauce used to promote Disney's Mulan
back when it was in its theatrical run. People began
demanding McDonald's bring back the sauce and, sensing
a situation in which they barely had to lift a finger,
McDonald's whipped them up into a frenzy. The lifestyle
and identity elements just occurred naturally; McDonald's
just had to show them how "pro-consumer" they were and
the grift commenced.

I would say I believe this to be a product of being
socialized in a society in which cultivation of identity by
capital is accepted as a social norm. I also believe that

when this happens, the resulting identity is still cultivated by capital, just indirectly.

When consumption is identity, others' creative work is *potential* identity. When it matures into cultivated identity, we treat others' creative work as *our property*. It stops being a house and becomes a home. Have you ever had someone criticize your home? It doesn't feel good, and it causes us to do all sorts of messed-up shit.

We wouldn't admit to operating that way, because we don't really think we do… But we do. Let's say you rent your home. You're asked to pay rent, then, right? Of course.

So, you know how every single year we're told "we need everyone to buy _____ so we can keep making them" in reference to your favorite thing? This is a statement reminding those people who have invested their identity in the product to *pay up or else*.

If your landlord really wanted to, the bastard could unlock your door and leave a goat heart on your kitchen counter at night. You could probably get litigious, but if your landlord did that, I doubt they care. The point was to remind you who actually owns the place.

"We don't have to let you live here. We don't care if this is your home, we own it" is a contradictory message to "we need you to buy this so that we can continue to make things and you can briefly feel whole!" Essentially, we're being told we're needed as well as not needed.

Given that cultivated identity is fragile and incomplete, delivering contradictory messages only serves to further confound a person already on edge with who they are. This only works to the advantage of those doing the cultivation. The more vulnerable a person's identity is, the more likely the person is to hyperconsume. To obsessively buy everything, read everything, to fixate and aggressively advocate. Whether they advocate for or against the product itself is quite irrelevant, it's simply the attention it receives and how cultivators invest that attention. A massive backlash might sound negative, but it does heighten awareness a great deal. If the marketing department knows what they're doing, they can use that attention to buy hype. "We want to thank the real fans for sticking with us. They mean everything to us and are so awesome for believing in us. We only want to give them the best product possible."

Normal consumption is *a* goal, for sure, but a subset of hyperconsumers is *the* goal. They're the most reliable and most sizable revenue stream. Someone with a life centered around consumption of a brand (and the lifestyle it's positioned with) will do more word-of-mouth advocacy on behalf than a team of marketers can even think to accomplish. They'll innovate marketing in a way thought leaders in making will never begin to dream of. They only care about how to sell something, and not about the minutiae of the actual artistic work; fans care about that deeply.

When one's identity is consumptive, then what the subject of their consumption becomes very important to that person. Their interpretation of those works is a central tenant to who they believe they are as a person. Certainly, the philosophies of artists of all kinds have bearing on this and in all people who consume their work, but we're talking on another level. The fact that consumption (particularly of creative work) affects identity is not the problem. The issue I am attending to the is that when consumption effectively takes over the main functions of identity, it leads to obsessive and/or abusive behaviors that have been so publicly on display as of late.

Star Wars, Five Nights At Freddy's, Stranger Things, and Donald Trump - what do they have in common? Beyond their rabid fandoms (yes, Trump *absolutely* has a fandom), we view all of them as consumables. In a world that pushes consumption-as-identity as hard as ours does, everything must be one. This situation is the default to us. As we observe fandom, the "real fans" are the ones living this situation. It takes a lot of work on the part of marketers to make this reality so.

If everything can generate wealth, then everything is a business. If wealth can be measured socially as well as economically, then we don't have to look at physical "products" as our way of generating wealth, nor do we have to provide a service. Something merely has to exist and do whatever it is expected to be consumed in this situation. It's possibly most gross when we view people as consumables, but so many people think that being a "personality" is something to aspire to, where do we even start?

Framing everything as consumption, everyone as consumers or consumables, and everything said or made as consumables is made possible by cultivating identity around it to defend this situation. The opposite is also true; the cultivation of identity is possible in such a widespread manner because everything is looked at as a consumable. Changing this situation means changing a person's custom reality, which *feels* the same as if you turned gravity off or made all the air into water.

But if you're on gravity's side, every day you wake up not floating in a pressureless void is validation.

PETER COFFIN

10. BEAUTY AND ROT

But why? We've talked about, among other things, ideology that co-opts the fact we are all unique individuals, metaphorical markets for discourse and fact, and corporations carving themselves out a place in our inner selves with the intention of getting us to consume more.

Now let's talk about Star Wars.

I've brought up 2017's *The Last Jedi* a few times, but I think there's much more to glean from it in the context of "custom reality." The user reviews are a pretty good case study in attempting to manipulate reality. In a galaxy far, far away, we were treated to a Luke Skywalker who had cut himself off from the outside, desperately regretting the past. We saw several different perspectives of the event he regretted, in which the impetus and deed were descriptively the same but came off very differently.

At first, we saw the version Luke wished he remembered, then we got Kylo Ren's version—the perspective of a kid who woke up one night not sure if his uncle would kill him—and then the version in which Luke admits his wrongdoing, but still a different perspective from Ren's. The movie itself acknowledges perspective changes with environment, but it was the reaction to the movie itself that I find of particular interest.

Opposition to the film came from a cross-section of Real Fans™ who felt deeply hurt by the lack of ability to consume an exact replica of *The Empire Strikes Back*, as well as from reactionaries, people who are angry that society continues to change. Groups of both took to Rotten Tomatoes' user reviews section, typically writing that the movie's story was too much of a departure, that it was too humorous, or that they didn't like its progressive politics. Then many of them repeated the action several times, either manually or using a bot or script.

Rotten Tomatoes has claimed this didn't happen, though they are under no obligation to acknowledge if it did. In fact, the very idea of a law concerning transparency in what amounts to a comment section is somewhat laughable. There's no such thing as a content company that doesn't absolve itself from liability regarding user interactions in their terms of service. But if they did acknowledge that this happened, it would undermine the validity of one of the more popular features on their site. There's neither incentive nor requirement for them to do so, though, so why would they?

One user operating a Facebook group called "Down With Disney's Treatment of Franchises and Fanboys" claimed his bot malfunctioned and posted some reviews of *The Last Jedi* on *The Shape of Water* instead. I can think of very few other reasons for the reviews saying they were angry about Luke being portrayed "badly" by "harming men" and lack of an explanation about who Snoke is in the user review section for that film. *The Shape of Water* was clearly under no obligation to reveal Supreme Leader Snoke's backstory.

Actual film critics saw it differently. Though, by this point in the book, I hope that when you read the phrase "actual film critics," a little voice in the back of your head says, "*some* are legitimate experts, and *some* are thought leaders trying to round up a validation gang." I don't want people to think that just because one gets paid to critique films automatically makes one a great film critic. Still, "actual" film critics typically had much more positive opinions of the film. What almost all of them negatively criticized, however, was a plot thread where several characters go to an opulent city called Canto Bight on a planet called Cantonica.

I'll summarize this part of the movie:

Two rebels must sabotage a large ship. To do this, they'll need to sneak aboard, and to get aboard, they'll need clearance codes, which change every hour. To even have a small chance, they must recruit a master code breaker. There is one apparently hanging out in a Canto Bight casino, so they go there.

They improperly park on arrival, then get to see, firsthand, both the relative beauty that wealth creates and the sickening exploitation that enables it. One of the two rebels has a more detailed understanding of why these people are rich, telling a story of oppression in a mining operation, as well as pointing out that the casino's patrons are mainly in the business of selling weapons to the First Order, the *evil* owners of the very ship they need to sabotage. But before they can speak to him, they are arrested for having parked improperly earlier. Should have thought that through!

In jail, they meet another code breaker who is, let's say, significantly less cut from the cloak of a traditional "hero." He seems very much like he could even be *a problem*, but he is also the only option as there isn't much chance they will see the other code breaker again from behind bars. Reluctantly, they recruit him, then escape in a manner that trashes the casino and frees some abused space horses that are raced for fun and profit.

On the way to their final objective, the shady code breaker reveals that the weapons' dealers also do business with The Resistance (the good guys), and that business people really don't care about what is designated as "good" or "bad," rather, their main concern is that money is flowing in their direction. This ultimately is his personal stance as well; he sells out the mission when he finds out they've been caught. They are unable to sabotage their enemy and the mission is a failure, leaving The Resistance in one hell of a pickle.

To some, the lack of a payoff in the form of a massive victory is regarded as a lack of a point. I disagree; I believe this part of the movie is meant to be an imitation of (possibly even homage to) the films Studio Ghibli. If you were to take that part of the movie out and watch it as a standalone, it would play like a brisk Ghibli film of the earlier, more bleak variety. Serendipity and chaos combine to free the space horses and trash the casino, but then things don't go the same way when the code breaker who is mainly concerned with profit sells them up the river.

There is an obvious point, though. I think more than one, in fact. The first is that failure isn't the end; we should learn from both our successes and failures. This is, ultimately, the point of the movie and not having a sequence that provides context in the way Canto Bight does would lessen the amount of sense the film makes. However, I think this more general point is ignored due to a more specific point this sequence makes.

That point is "systems of profit don't have a 'side,' but ultimately the worst people tend to have more money, so these systems help them more." Hoarding wealth is on a pretty short list of "definitely bad" traits and is rarely the only one checked off when it is. Rian Johnson, co-writer and director of *The Last Jedi*, seems as though he wanted to make this clear. This showed that the rebels aren't just up against space fascists, but that there are people who benefit from the prolonged conflict between these two sides. This applies not only to the arms dealers in the fictional galaxy of Star Wars, but also to the non-fictional company that made the movie, Disney. Neither fictional nor non-fictional parties involved are interested in progressing beyond the conflict because the conflict is profitable.

Most importantly, it showed that someone with good in their heart and the best of intentions can think a place is cool and great because they don't understand that the mold has been painted over. The beauty of Canto Bight was on full display in its architecture, a mixture of Dubrovnik, Croatia, amazing practical set design, and CGI augmentation. We were given the ability to see much of the city from a bird's eye view, a blunt way of saying "from a distance this seems amazing." The closer we get to things that seem wondrous, though, the material cost becomes much clearer. There are child slaves and those space horses I mentioned have huge scars from the abuse they suffer on an ongoing basis. Sadly, this is the nature of the world *we* inhabit, as well. We often can look away, though, because of our ability to choose to stay at a distance. *The Last Jedi* did not give us a choice, and it made a point that hits a bit too close for comfort.

The beauty hides the rot. A beautiful veneer must obstruct the rot, or the rot will be scrutinized.

The rebels are not just fighting an analog for Nazis and all their evil. They're also fighting an analog for capital interests, which don't appear to be outright evil. In fact, everyone is supposed to aspire to get into that position. The fascists are indeed the greatest threat, but the fight against them is profitable and therefore profiteers will seek to prolong it. This is also a likely contributing factor to the failure of the New Republic, the government that was organized after the Empire was destroyed in *Return of the Jedi*. This unending conflict where the answer, already very apparent, yet profitable to avoid, should seem familiar.

It's the Marketplace of Ideas, but in space.

Setting up a hasty New Republic after the old one proved that competing interests inevitably position it for a charismatic fascist to take power, either through subversion of its marketplace of ideas or by force, due to the utter lack of preparation of a defense, seems like an obviously bad idea. Simply duplicating previous systems that are proven vulnerable to the rise of fascism will, y'know, cause fascism to rise. We just didn't get three less-liked movies about the failure of bureaucracy this time around.

By my thoughts, these points I mention about the film fit pretty well into what I believe the overall theme of the film to be, which is to keep what works and leave behind what doesn't. It's about acknowledgement of the flaws in heroes and legends and understanding that, while they may have some of the answers, they do not have them all. It asserts that we must embrace change because nothing is permanent. Not who we are, not where we are, and certainly not how we see things. It asks us to understand the beauty and the rot, and it demands that we seek to end the rot. Without the rot, the performative beauty is no longer needed to uphold the situation, and will be washed away. What doesn't matter won't survive, but any beauty that *does* survive will be of a totally different kind.

Permanence is an illusion, much like objectivity, and I'd assert these things are extremely related. When we see something as permanent, we tend to neglect that it needs maintenance. When we see reality as objective, we do the same. These are things we are in dire need of hearing, and to see them depicted in a blockbuster film was something I did not expect. The idea that we need to examine what we were socialized to believe and address the paradoxes that have arisen is a fairly radical one, though it should be looked at as *absolutely amazing we've designed a world where reflection is radical.*

Film critics acted as though the Canto Bight part of the movie, the part which discussed the systemic problems the theme of the film points at, was just pointlessly included and therefore not very enjoyable. I feel that on some level, this is an unconscious reaction to being told the system we live in is, itself, *the problem.* Remember that these critics, among many others in the media, depend on this system to survive as much as they do to thrive.

Now, I could tell you about why I liked that part of the movie, but honestly, I think it would only prove that part of my identity is that of a Star Wars Fan™. I think it serves better to say that despite all my talk, I still know what it feels like to be excited for a movie to come out. The movie also acted as an outlet for other wants of mine, including its surprisingly harsh criticism of capitalism (at least for a mainstream blockbuster) that people seem not to want to acknowledge is there—instead calling it "pointless." I have reasons to be interested in this film; in many ways it feels like it was made *for me*, and that sounds rather like "cultivated identity." I have no qualms in saying that it very well could be. *That's the point of the book. It's all of us.*

This part of the movie serves to contextualize the rest of the movie (and all other Star Wars movies) with the idea that everything *you are* is useful to capital, though. You can become a commodity by having your humanity stripped from you just as easily as validating it. It doesn't matter if you're a screaming fascist or "rebel scum," profit can be had. The same people are benefiting either way.

Karl Marx was *okay* at predictions. He had failures (he asserted that capitalism would just naturally evolve into socialism... ha) and successes (he predicted automation in his writings from 1857). He even used the term "social capital." He meant something different by it than how we use it now, saying it to mean "the total amount of capital society possesses."

In fact, he never predicted anything like what we have labeled "social capital." When we say the term today, we are referring to the commodification of things such as credibility and trust.

To follow this line of thinking, in our neoliberal, heavily marketized society, you could say we have "social capitalism." Now, this term has been used to describe a theoretical "in between" for socialism and capitalism, but here I'm using it to say that *social* capitalists do all the same shit that *economic* capitalists do. Except their market is one of ideas and the currency they traffic in is attention. They trade it for social commodities—credibility and trust—and hoard that wealth and any other wealth created in the process.

I believe this to be the logical conclusion of socializing generation after generation to believe a set of norms that tug them in many different directions at once, in the name of extracting value from them. We are the ultimate authority on everything and cannot be wrong, but we are also fragile and unconfident in our infallibility. Everything is our fault, good or bad, and when things are bad, we just didn't work hard enough. How could anyone think that would never bleed in to our behavior socially? Our environment will forever change and therefore demands a continually developing version of human nature. Our actions will always become second nature *in a second nature*. The environment will require us to interface with it differently, to develop new behaviors, and to understand we must define emergent ideas and means of existence.

The desire to rule is the incentive to manipulate reality. We do not live in a monarchy, however, so how does one "rule" in capitalism?

The social side of capitalism acts as the infrastructure to "rule." If you "have all the answers," you can sell access to them. You can deal in monetary capital or social capital, but either way you're going to ultimately gain share in the Marketplace of Ideas to truly "rule" in some capacity. People must believe that what you do is necessary and correct. They must "buy it," and they may honestly have to do so before *you* "buy it." You may have to "fake it 'til you make it."

So, much of our environment is intended to appear beautiful as it disguises the rot; the Canto Bight storyline in *The Last Jedi* lays that out plainly. One of the rebels verbalizes his wonder at the elegance of the place, only to be rebuked by the other's story I mentioned earlier. The point of individualizing reality is to avoid people getting angry enough to band together, free the space horses, and trash the casino.

Why must we be led to think things are beautiful when they are rotting? Well, people who are selling something are always *very* positive. So, are we all supposed to be selling something?

Our economic system is a large-scale value extraction operation. You are being asked to sell the idea that it's fair, both to yourself and to others. You're asked to look in the mirror and sell yourself on giving it your all today, even if you hate doing it. You're asked to show up at work and act like this project is *awesome*, to sell the idea that things are *awesome here* and that things here *work out awesome*. You're supposed to believe student debt is a fact of life and the idea that profiting from healthcare isn't one of the worst things you've ever heard. You're supposed to think racism isn't worth talking about in a systemic capacity and that there is no wage gap. Hell, you're not supposed to even really think about what wages *really are*.

If we look at this false positivity as a false reality, we must start to see this as a means, but to what? What is the motive? How do you rule in capitalism? What do you need? What do you want? What might you already have if you are in the position to acquire more?

It must be profit.

Profit is the incentive for keeping every lie we live with active. It's the incentive to own and control the environment in which we make choices. It's the incentive to make everything as cheaply as possible and instead sell the product on the nice things the brand is associated with over time. If they don't control the environment, if you don't believe your first decision based on the first information you receive is the correct one, if they don't find a way around scrutiny, then all the garbage they do (selling cheap crap made by slave or near-slave labor) *brings trouble to their door.*

Profit is what racists receive when they make other racists feel good for being racist. I promise you that donations to Richard Spencer's think tank went up after Heather Heyer's death in Charlottesville at the hands of a white supremacist. I also promise you white supremacists were enriched in terms of social capital when the President of the United States said there were "fine people on both sides" in regard to an incident where white supremacists got together and killed a protestor.

Profit is what I, someone condemning profit, *will receive myself* if this book is a "success." Oh yes, I'm not going to sit here and pretend that isn't possible. My motives for making this book are not to get rich, nor do I believe it will result in that. But it *could* happen. That would be weird; to pay off debts, to own a home, to know my family wouldn't struggle for the duration. When the world changes, would it matter?

I'm an individual. I pay rent. I eat food. I have bills and debt. This system sucks, and I am at the mercy of it, at least as much as most people. While there are people who have it worse than I do, I'm not rich. My family lives on a working-class income. I surely don't believe this book will make me rich. I believe it will get into a few people's hands and illustrate an easily understandable version of the framework I think is being used to keep us at bay.

I am dumping all of this into the Marketplace of Ideas, the very construct I have pointed at as a big part of the problem, hoping that what I'm saying finds its way to enough people so that it can begin to undo it. Such a ridiculous metaphor, ultimately constructed so some may profit in some way, might start to see more opponents. Hopefully some people who are stronger, smarter and better at organizing people than myself.

Social profit brings economic profit. Economic profit brings social profit. Someone with social and economic capital has the means to lobby more effectively than anyone else and, therefore, is more likely to affect actual laws. Much of this is more roundabout and requires those with agenda to get their ducks in a row, but it brings about real power and control. Because we believe in a "Marketplace of Ideas" where every side is valid, we often think of fence-sitting as "being critical of both sides." The Golden Mean is a logical fallacy, though, and this view invites those with bad faith arguments (often debunked ones) the ability to insert themselves into many discussions in which they otherwise have no business.

This can be subverted; in fact, we've seen it happen very recently. The weakness that Trump exploited is the same one that Hitler and Mussolini did—they just happened to be doing it on purpose as part of a plan. The First Order even did it in the Star Wars novel Claudia Gray wrote called *Bloodline*. A faction of the New Republic *actually* called the "Centrists" was subverted by the First Order to cause political deadlock and unrest.

Trump is just a jackass. That's not to say a jackass isn't a threat; people like him have eroded these constructs for many years. But with Trump, it's not 4D chess. He's just naturally the thing that works when you have a system like this, where people are becoming discontent without access to understanding why. Loud strongmen will scapegoat just about anything, and when money controls access, the poor are kept away from the full story. This is why framing any information situation as a market is bad. Trump didn't even have to understand it and he's President.

In competitive situations, profit often requires cutting corners and engaging in practices that harm the world simply because they advance the interest of growth. Physical commodities markets are manipulated for the sake of acquiring more capital. We should stop pretending this only applies to the material and the physical, though. As if people wouldn't do that, even if doing so made them more money. Sure! As if there are no people out there who understand that attention is another form of money. I bet! As if no capitalists attempt to expand influence and reach. I believe that! As if they have no incentive to. Okay, this is more sad than funny!

Media outlets profit when they present the views that validate their viewers. Capital profit when their advertisements have an effect. Profit works best when people perceive the extraction of value from commodities, time, and themselves as "normal." Unfortunately, that is exactly how it is viewed.

Everything must change, because it all eventually comes down to profit. The incentive to strategically falsify what people perceive, as to engineer a desired outcome, really is the basis of our system today. The most basic monetary model for the art we all enjoy is advertising, and many people consider it harmless, even if a little irritating. However, advertising is *perception management*. I'll quickly allow the harmlessness of that phrase to pass and wait for your realization that this means "control over the environment in which you make choices."

We accept it *on a constant basis*. Advertising is ever-present. From the obvious commercials and billboards to the subtler product placement or brand integrations we see on YouTube or even in movies, it's an attempt to engineer your actions. Most of the time it works, even when you think you're above it. People accept this as a fact of life, but it truly is the most omnipresent version of what this book is about. Advertising is the most blatant form of reality manipulation, and though it is the least effective, it is very effective.

When you don't realize it's happening, though, that's when it works best. Earlier, I mentioned Edward Bernays's book *Propaganda*, in which he had an interesting way of saying this:

> *A store which seeks a large sales volume in cheap goods will preach prices day in and day out, concentrating its*

whole appeal on the ways in which it can save money for its clients. But a store seeking a high margin of profit on individual sales would try to associate itself with the distinguished and the elegant, whether by an exhibition of old masters or through the social activities of the owner's wife.

The perception of elegance and the associated lifestyle function here as the beauty. The fact that a product that is no more materially useful bears a higher price and, therefore, a higher margin, is the rot.

The PGA golf club and the world-class hotel in Benton Harbor, Michigan, built in the last decade as a certain multinational corporation continues to gentrify the city, are certainly beautiful. They have their world HQ in a city that is 89% black and 60% of its residents live at or below the poverty line. They have a page on their website about how diverse they are, but I can't help wondering how many local people they hire. They will not be mentioned by name, though, because I could see that getting litigious and I would like not to have a multinational corporation on my ass. It's not a tough guess, though.

The company was founded by some rich folks. The wealth they put into it is literally nothing compared to what it's worth today. They have an heir to that fortune, too. But not just any rich kid doing nothing; he is also a member of the US Congress. He might even represent the district Benton Harbor is in—who knows? This company is known for doing anything it can to utilize tax loopholes, and this gentleman voted "yes" on the unpopular tax bill Donald Trump signed on December 22nd, 2017. It's hard for me to figure out why, though!

Benton Harbor borders a river, which flows into Lake Michigan. On the river, the city is beautiful—new buildings in the business district and expensive homes closer to the lake's beach. There's an airport where private jets land. It's a very convenient way to get to the golf course. According to Facebook posts, Leonardo DiCaprio was there once last year. So cool!

Elsewhere, though, memories of police killing unarmed black people remain. It's too easy for some folks to forget things like that. For the people close to it, however, it's always there. Terrance Shurn was speeding on his motorcycle when he was run off the road after police "bumped" into him (according to multiple witnesses). You know, because death is an appropriate punishment for speeding. Then there's Arthur Partee, who was choked to death outside his home while being arrested for a traffic violation.

There's a dismal mall if you travel several miles in, clearly given up on. The parking lot is overgrown due to a total lack of maintenance, reminiscent of a post-apocalyptic film. Inside it isn't much better; the majority of it is unrented and the few stores still occupied look very lonely.

Decades ago, this city was run dry, and now a multinational corporation is "saving it." Sure, it looks nice in certain areas, but where is that value being extracted from? Letting the place rot to a husk was a great way to ensure real estate was extremely low, and then the state swooped in to enact an "emergency manager" system. This very same system was also enacted in Flint, Michigan, where two former emergency managers have been indicted on felony charges regarding their water crisis.

The way that system works: the state appoints a manager to the city to essentially act in the way a corporate manager would operate if the city was a business. Decisions made by democratically elected city officials could be (and were) overridden in favor of the state's will, which for decades has mainly functioned to enrich Michigan businesses.

Speaking of the state, two former aides of that one heir-turned-politician I mentioned went on to government positions in Michigan. One is a State Senator and one is the state's budget director. I can't see how that would benefit that multinational corporation. Obviously, it is *plausible* that I got positions wrong or possibly even the whole scenario, so I will say that I would *deny* anything specific if asked.

We often hope that our government will pass rules to stop people from acting in a manner that harms the public good, but ultimately this harm is just a fact of life where those with power work only to extract value. This is the point of our system, and ultimately the government doesn't work against it *at all*. The government is *for* this, partly because taxes fund the government and partly because these corporations basically have representatives *in the government* working to fortify their position. They act as a support system, so these corporations can "save" cities in a similar way as described here.

How are we in the dark about how this all happened? Well, Canto Bight *is* beautiful...

PETER COFFIN

11. SEIZE YOURSELF

I woke up today with the desire to sleep some more. I almost always do; my wife and I have two kids and they don't sleep until noon (for whatever reason). One is only a few months old as I write this book, and my sleep schedule is anything but stable.

During the day, everything is more obvious and present. But during the night, it takes effort to see. What lights you turn on determine what your house looks like. It's a bit as if your home is a canvas and light is paint.

How you light your home is a simple exercise in artistic interpretation. I like less harsh lighting, personally. I've also just *got to* have faders. Whatever your preference, however, everything is still there. The dark and the quiet don't erase things; they just limit your perception of them.

Our relationship to the universe is comparable to this; at times, it is easier to see than others. Conditions change and with them our perception.

Night to the human eye makes objects take on another form. As shadows become slightly deeper and ominous, we become slightly less rational. We seem to have embedded worry in darkness and associate it with uncertainty. In the night, things that we declare "totally impossible" during the day are sometimes a question. What if ghosts are real? What if this house is haunted? What if my antique doll collection springs to life and goes on a rampage?

Side note: that last one is *your fault* if it ever somehow happens. Anyone with any ounce of sense would not have an antique doll collection, for multiple reasons.

These aren't things I believe in at all. I think they're silly, and I think it's foolish to believe in them. That said, I don't think the people who believe in the supernatural are fools; the right set of circumstances can make many things seem real.

One may be raised in an environment where authority is openly abused, so there isn't much trust in information that comes from authority. Or one might be tired and prone to nightmares ever since they kept replacing their own face with hellish deformations by intentionally using Snapchat improperly. I'm not saying I'm definitely the latter, but I might be. I really might.

As much as I have personally made up my mind on the supernatural, *I could be wrong*. Sure, I'm confident in what I think on this subject. But I am not a god myself; to claim omnipresence would basically invalidate my belief structure. I'm fallible, as are you. Our perception makes us prone to believe things differently.

Besides artistic interpretation, the way you light your home at night is also the application of power, and in more than one sense. To use "power" as a synonym for electricity, you're using up potential energy generated and stored to be bought and sold as a commodity. You purchase it and gain power over how it is used. Using "power" to mean "to direct or influence the behavior of others or the course of events," you are exerting your will on your direct surroundings to change it as you see fit.

For me, the most interesting thing about the concept of an individualized, custom reality is that we're creating one for whether we're doing it responsibly or irresponsibly. Also, while it may seem like we're doing it specifically for ourselves and our own benefit, we're being directed and guided so that others may benefit.

In fact, one could call reality the main product that humanity's labor produces. Some say that the meaning of life is "to create meaning," but what is meaning? Whether we mean to indicate interpretation, significance or essence, we're talking about the reality of one's situation. Should we die out and another species find the remains of our civilization, they will attempt to put together an idea of how we lived. Assuming they cared about archaeology, their understanding of our reality would consider evidence, such as carbon dating of fossils and the cycles of organic matter, but it would also be very dependent on our records. We could "spin" our history as a species of whosoever we desired. I doubt very much that our current history is a genuine "no spin zone," and in that context, the effect of custom reality could be observed perhaps a little easier.

This should act as evidence of the power one has in artistic interpretation. If it matters enough that we want to change something as materially unimportant as lighting based on one's own personal preferences, it matters that events that happened long ago are remembered a certain way. It's important we recognize that artistic interpretation is a form of labor, and thus an exertion of power on the world. All of one's interpretation is artistic. The exertion of your ideas and ideals into the medium of your choice, conscious or not, is your art. In many ways, the current nightmare that is "reality" is the work of many different, deviously creative "artists." They just do not paint *with paint*.

The brush they use to paint their masterpiece works from a palette of commodities, and I don't just mean the basic earth tones of wood brown, water blue or coal black. I'm referring to more cerebral, challenging colors like brain peach and heart mauve. Everything has become a commodity.

Your smile is regarded as a commodity. When a seemingly well-intentioned man tells a woman she should smile, it's because he doesn't view this stranger as a person. He wants to consume her smile, as well as consume his ability to make her do it. He views their passing glance as a transaction and the dancing monkey must dance. At the same time, he views her face as a canvas and her smile as his creation. He's looking to *consume the experience of creating something he does not actually create* and, again, the customer is always right.

This is *the expectation of all possible actions and outcomes* as a commodity. While this isn't a feature that appeared thanks to neoliberalism, the ideology provides a way to perpetuate and propagate it. We have been conditioned to expect this; we are Pavlov when we have power and we are his dog when we don't. It's not always easy to tell who we are, but this is a closed system, keeping the small folk in a small struggle with other small folk.

The climate I have described here is how I believe power is exerted over us in a manner that compensates for the fact we are all, in this respect, an "artist." I will be the first to admit that I am human and that this reality is my product; I am imperfect and this could be wrong. But if this works as I believe it does, it is either brilliant or the most amazing accident that's ever happened. Rather than trying to thwart this inner desire to interpret and create, even on the smallest of scales, it nurtures those abilities while directing them into undertakings that aid (or at least can't interfere with) the system and its pilots' goal: money, power and control. It works, too.

But as an individual, if you understand that it is happening, you can also say "fuck that." And it needs to be said as we collectivize, or those collectives are doomed.

If you've read this book and been made angry, good. Not just good, incredible. We need to be pissed off, and that's all on you, my friend. Though we can *share* anger as a group, we can only *feel* it as individuals. People either get angry when they see injustice, or they don't. I hope I'm pushing you towards the former.

I feel angry about how this works. It's a scheme so clever that it predicts the attempt to inspire others to figure it out and engineers a response to thwart scrutiny. I can't tell you how to feel, but if you've made it to this point I have a feeling you might agree. Which means you'll probably want to stop it.

You'll want to tell people, "you're being tricked!" Not only will that be ineffective because of the identity the various forces of capital have so carefully cultivated in those who do not actively shield themselves, and the ever-growing demand to be perpetually correct, *but people legitimately aren't being tricked.*

We have been groomed.

Individually speaking, we must take ourselves back from that socialization, from this environment. I make the distinction between individualism and individuality because that battle is so utterly internal. We all must individually beat the co-option of "the empowerment of the individual." We must break free from *the results* of egoist thinking, where the individual's agency becomes our ultimate authority, creating the perception that what one knows now is exactly enough. Everything that *sounds* good must no longer *be* automatically good; investigation may sound like a questioning of one's authority but who is even exercising it? It's certainly not us, no matter what it feels like.

We must fully grasp the concept of environmental control and that it results in the ability to engineer consent. This is what Edward Bernays was on about; it works kind of like passive aggression if it were applied to the full landscape of society. The result is an environment of omitted facts, carefully curated norms, selective oversimplification, over-complication, distractions, misinformation and other issues.

The individual should not be made disenfranchised by the collective. That's not the point of working together in any way. We do not carpool so that we may be disenfranchised, we do it so that we might save some cash and put a bit less smoke in the air. We do it to have someone to talk to before we step into the value extraction machine. We do it because we have friends and we care about them. We don't do it to control each other, at least hopefully not.

That's not to say a carpool couldn't be used as a means of environmental control. Almost anything can be authoritarian, and that's why when we talk about collectivizing, we need to talk about it in a less scary way.

9/11 in some ways collectivized us in a bad way. It terrified many of us, and it is one of many reality windshield-breaking rocks that we haven't properly dealt with. Among other things, we need to learn how to tell others about this without blaming them for it, too.

The concepts I've attempted to define and criticize in this book are, regardless of intent, used to funnel wealth and power upward. There's always been a class of people who have more and other classes with less. We live in a system that uses the haves/have-nots dynamic to survive and thrive, *but those pesky poors and minorities keep banding together to demand a less hellish experience for themselves.*

Collectivization is what happens when people start expressing the scrutiny they have personally applied to things. They speak with other people around them and the illusion capital has worked to construct crumbles. This can happen at family get-togethers where people share that this supposedly great product simply sucks in their opinion. It also happens in the news as powerful men get outed as sexual harassers and abusers. When evidence is corroborated, the selective omissions made in the prevalent narrative can be made clear. There's no guarantee it will, but instead of just claiming something to be true, would it not be better to… work on it? We small folk could, in theory, stop using what we "know" as a bludgeon against the smaller folk with even less, individuals will begin working together. We could side with each other rather than with capital and a government that seems to exist purely to enable them.

We're meant to consider the decisions we make as unquestionably correct because it was our decision. It is an exercise of our judgement of whether or not something presented to us smells of bull, and our value as a person is tied to it. However, there's no situation any person will ever see in which they have all the information immediately. Even less are the situations where all the information is spoon-fed without active investigation and research. Media companies have tried to make it look like that is their job and that they are doing it... But it isn't and they're not.

We must all be more skeptical, and this has to have less to do with who we are and more to do with the methodology of how we look at things. As much as I believe the societal solution is collectivizing, corroborating, and otherwise working together, that isn't to say we don't have our internal issues to work on. We were socialized in *this* world, and we will carry the social norms of the current world wherever we go.

You, as an individual, may also need to work out the difference between being skeptical and being "a skeptic" and you need to act accordingly. Whether you do or do not consider yourself to be "a skeptic," that idea that one must do so *to be skeptical* is something that needs to be left in the past. You do not need the label of skepticism, though I am not going to shame you if indeed you take it on. What I ask is that regardless of what you call yourself, you act genuinely skeptical. I personally think it's more productive not to take it on as an identity, but I'm not going to tell you that everything is as cut-and-dry as the words on these pages. The lines are much blurrier. If they weren't, there would be no need for anyone to say anything.

gnizant of the idea that an individual and a
can be at odds. It must also be said that the
_on of evidence becomes an argument to
authority with only one step in logic. We are a species that
happily argues about what is rational without
acknowledging that the universe isn't. We made up
"rational." Nothing about the universe should be regarded
this way; instead, it should be regarded as something
foreign to human understanding.

The ideology of individualism leads us down the
corridors of a prison that presents itself as voluntary but a
collective cannot be authoritarian. We are creating our own
custom realities on an individual level but must attempt to
corroborate these realities with others. Acceptance of
evidence is simultaneously authoritative and, if done
responsibly, the path to liberation from narrative created
by those in power.

I don't want to resolve this contradiction, I want to lean
the hell into it. We are a contradiction ourselves, an
intelligent animal, the organic industrialists. We are trying
to resolve an unsolvable paradox instead of acknowledging
it and working to create a good situation. We must
understand what individualism gets us and thus what to
avoid, but should work as hard as we can to make a
situation that empowers us all as individuals and as groups.

We should not be *easily* convinced of anything. Yes, that
does mean looking at everything with a question in mind.
It also means looking at previous answers to questions
skeptically. Though, many that currently call themselves
"skeptics" take this to mean that one must just outright
reject all answers. I believe that is a cop-out *at the very best*.
What I am saying is that one must investigate all answers
and *take evidence seriously*. That means collaboration and
substantiation, an embrace of good faith and an
unambiguous rejection of bad faith and those acting in it.
I'm talking everything from "don't accept assertions at face
value" to "don't accept evidence that, on peer-review, was

debunked." There's a contradiction to embrace here, one that I hope in future work to make something of: there is no current right answer on how to do this. The contradiction puts us all at a crossroads where we either accept information from an authority or ask every individual to essentially live a life of endless research, something that is not a logical or respectful thing to ask of people. Life is short.

Our current process is often *described very similarly,* but the he mechanics of our current system deviate significantly. This book doesn't contain discussion on the Marketplace of Ideas and related constructs for no reason; it's important to remember that if we frame discourse this way, we don't talk about finding answers, we talk about *choosing our answers* and *pitting those answers against each other in endless competition.*

An argument should not continue just because the market demands it, and you should not accept this mode of operation. You are not obliged to engage with people trying to argue disproven points, nor is a school obliged to platform Charles Murray, whom the Southern Poverty Law Center, whom I am now deferring to as an authority, describes as such:

> *Charles Murray, a fellow at the American Enterprise Institute, has become one of the most influential social scientists in America, using racist pseudoscience and misleading statistics to argue that social inequality is caused by the genetic inferiority of the black and Latino communities, women and the poor.*

The "truth" of this situation is that many people believe they should push schools to invite and platform people who deal in information that has been disproven in good faith, and agreeably labelled "bigoted." The people who believe in the stuff Murray says are usually people who feel validated by said information and work to get it accepted in any way possible.

Are you a part of any of these kinds of validation gangs? Well, maybe not exactly *this* kind. I hope you haven't read this far in a book I've written and actually take eugenics seriously. But you probably are part of *some* kind of validation gang. I very likely am, too. I think a lot of my behavior as a Star Wars fan over the years has been in the more benign areas of what we are talking about. I know things from Star Wars have mattered too much to me as a person at times in my life, though I certainly have never attacked anyone over it, and have worked to create a healthier version of my engagement with it. Star Wars will probably always do something magical for me, and I really don't think we should want to kill things like that. I hope there is something like that in everyone's lives.

Well, except Nazis. I wish they didn't have their "thing like that."

Creative work should affect us. We should care about what the message of art is, even if it ultimately isn't what we like about it. There is agenda in all creation and interpretation. We are lying to ourselves if we don't see this, and we're also lying to ourselves if we say that all agenda in art (or criticism) is bad. Message is motive *is agenda*, and there's no such thing as art that doesn't contain it. Even a blank canvas hung in an art gallery has an agenda. It could be for a laugh or to make a point about modern art. Or it could be modern art. I don't know.

The work of the individual in undoing their individualization of reality is counterintuitive and probably confusing.

A person must understand that our perception *is reality* for us. The thing we are describing as "reality," is simply the universe totally independent of human consciousness. We are always perceiving it through our imperfect, personal means. Everything we understand about it has been framed through human constructs. The first stop on the path to undoing the individualization and customization we've discussed is a revision of our societal conceptualization of reality itself.

Our social concept of reality that *is the underlying problem.* The Nasdaq stock market has never been higher, but people around the world have never been exploited on this level. To acknowledge this is to be doing more about it than the average person has ever done. Hell, even just saying the words "individualized custom reality" does more than saying the word "bubble." When you are distinctly defining the actual issue with words that point much more directly at the components of it, you are making the preliminary moves that lead to solving it.

People want to "know what they're up against," as the adage goes. They want this for a reason.

To become as literate as one can about the individualization of reality, then attempting to spread that literacy, sounds like a very small thing for an individual to do. It really does. But if the problem with reality is that it can become individualized, it is of the utmost importance that individuals become *savvy.* Today, as you read this book, this means you. Tomorrow, it means everyone who will listen.

The thing I've been steadily advocating for in this book is an evidence-based collective reality. This doesn't happen if you sit in your house and laugh at the smug condescension on display in commercials, knowing you are above it. Real progress on this frontier happens when you have in-depth conversations with people who are willing to listen to you about how we got to this bizarre dystopia.

Some may say the solutions exist purely in the material world, asking folks to stop talking about "abstract nonsense." I'd argue that what many label as "the abstract" *is also the material,* especially since the advent and popularization of the internet. The internet is the real world and vice versa. Reality is a product of our species, and therefore, our perception is a means of production.

We are the workers, the machines *and* the factory. We are also the consumers. On the internet, our production and our consumption are bought and sold as commodities; you don't want to know where your search history goes. This makes our consumption into production and our production into consumption. As we consume, we produce.

Karl Marx believed that our societies develop their defining characteristics through class struggle. His critique of capitalism holds that the ruling class(es), which own the means of production, exists in conflict with the lower class(es), who sell their labor in return for wages. Surplus value is extracted from them, as wages are less than the total value of labor sold to accommodate seeking of profit.

We need to seize ourselves. If neoliberal capitalism is going to look at everything as commodities, then every person's every action is labor, and every moment of our existence is the product. Value is extracted from us in that all of this reality is subjected to a canonization process that involves the various constructs we've discussed, in which those with power choose what works best for their bottom line.

What I am saying is that currently, we are dehumanized. We are not in a situation in which we can say "I am not a commodity. My ideas, thoughts, and feelings are not commodities. The idea of seizing oneself as the means of production of a commodified reality, is to rehumanize.

You must take *yourself* back; you were never given the option to opt-in to this. We were all born into this. This has always been "the world" for us. We must say "no, I do not accept this method or level of control."

If we revolt and overturn the unjust hierarchy without purging all of this from what we consider our personal canon, we may undermine ourselves in very serious ways. We may still be looking at the situation as untenable; we were raised to believe a wage is fair and that money is necessary. What if the society of the future has neither? How will you integrate into this situation?

I'll spare you the "we've got to unplug from the Matrix" kind of talk, because at this point you may understand that I'm not so keen on the opinion that "the Cyber is bad." Quite the contrary, I think the Cyber is good. I just happen to also think when wealth and power can be concentrated, those who have the technology will use it to reign.

We need to seize ourselves as the means to produce reality. We need to understand exactly what that means and how deep it runs. We must start in the neoliberal/capitalist framework we were all born into and socialized in. We must understand its conceits. If we start somewhere else, we're talking about goals. If we start where we are, we're talking about the path we walk. You need to take yourself back, find others, and we must collectivize.

The world is awash in contradiction, though, which is probably the most uncomfortable point I have to make to you. There is centrism, and then there is synthesis. There is fence-riding, and then there is nuance. It's not about balance, it's about the correct answer. But the correct answer becomes authority, and not everyone has the time or desire to follow a specific, rigorous process to verify claims. Are we asking those people to submit?

The point I make here is how much of a mess this all really is. How does one seize oneself when every element of freedom and authority is pulling in a different direction?

How do you pay rent when you separate your interests from that of capital? How do you reject environmental control while collecting a paycheck, an inherently coercive reward for allowing extraction of value from your labor? How can your mind be free when there's no way to free your body?

How can you reject the commodification of all things by saying "I am doing labor, I am creating a product" talking of perception and reality?

The answer to that is internal and abstract. A free mind acknowledges that a structure built to contain is inherent in the system, but a free mind is just one. It is one thing, one person and one step. We must care about individuals, including ourselves, without building a prison and calling it individualism. We build collectives for individuals, and individually care about the collective. It's not one or the other; the human condition is one of potential and our potential is abundant.

A free mind will search for an approach to free others, and many will disagree on which. We'll cite books, we'll argue about theory and it will be clear that we are a mess. Because that is what humanity is. But if we care about each other, then a mess is good.

When one seizes oneself, one becomes both a conduit and a current with too much voltage to handle running through it. One becomes a track and a train going recklessly fast on it. One embraces that our start point is neoliberal capitalism. We are here, not there. When one realizes they are one of many, many can become powerful by joining forces.

We embrace that we will be refuted, because to some, we look agents of chaos. This could very well be what you are, too. Is freedom chaos? Maybe. Can chaotic beings work together? I don't see why not; remember, "chaos" is a word; it is a thing humans made up.

To own your mind is the goal. This means taking it from those who own it now.

CUSTOM REALITY AND YOU

PETER COFFIN

12. CONCLUSION

The concepts I've discussed in this book are my conceptualization of what is going on in this world. My belief is that disagreements in what "the truth" is, subtle to significant, have slowly developed into a situation where we might as well all be living in different dimensions. This is a situation engineered and/or encouraged by capital interests.

If we aren't working not to, we will be trapped in our own, "perpetually correct" perspective, formed to preserve our perceived viability as a "productive human being" in a society where survival is a privilege to be earned. We are not at fault for this; it is the environment in which our upbringing takes place. It is a stronger, more effective, more accepted iteration of the same thing previous generations grew up in. What used to be called "keeping up with the Joneses" is now called "Instagram." Not that people are wrong for using social media; it's understandable why we do it. Where we are born and to whom are conditions in which we have absolutely no agency, much less in which socioeconomic system. It should not be our responsibility to understand this, explain it to others, or fight this; it isn't just. But someone must.

What does one do when identity is being cultivated as a crop? How does one belong when one refuses the false choices that yield a place that will accept them? What life is there for those who have walked away from a co-opted or pre-fabricated lifestyle and all the products and services associated with it?

I must confess, it's a bit scary. I won't pretend I'm hugely connected with a lot of people. I struggle with much of this; it's hard to feel as if you belong when you're not among friends in the stars, dressed up for the premiere, wearing the band merch, holding up a sign at a political rally. It's hard to know if any of this is truly real, or at least which parts of it.

What can one change? The key element in all of this is your ability to participate in this cycle of labor and consumption, and the requirement through coercive environmental control. We are led to believe that we are working towards becoming worthy (a "real fan"), or, for the less merit-oriented among us, we are working towards that place to belong. This is perception; when I say perception is reality and reality is your art, your being, and your product, it means you can change your output.

What one can change is their perception. I'm advocating that you perceive these constructs as simply another way of saying "you will work forever, you will give your time, your money, and your life to benefit a tiny class of people who make up well under 1% of the population. You will do this, and you will love it, obsessively, or you will starve."

Simply understanding how the human brain interprets its surroundings is a legitimate start point. For us all, it means overcoming the pushes to separate, which are inherent in the situation described, whether it's into demographics or down to "rational" self-interest, and becoming more of a genuine community. For one, this means the showdown debates about class and identity some like to have, need to stop. These aren't "sides," they are categories of concern. Poor white people are tyrannized because they're poor. Poor black people are tyrannized because they're poor and because they're black. Apply that to any identity or class. It's not that hard to get; it doesn't invalidate anyone's experience, especially if you understand the division simply hurts us while building our obstacles higher. I'm simplifying, but while we all must confront where we stand in hierarchies of marginalization, I'd suggest it would be better to stop arguing "what kind of politics works" and start understanding that the problems of one are the problems of all.

Identity is incredibly significant, otherwise powerful forces would not work so tirelessly to create an environment that defines it in a way that gives access to it. Why would a system want a means to direct identity if it wasn't valuable? Can a system created by people reach a level that doesn't require the intent of people to act? Capitalism is working at peak efficiency when it is extracting all kinds of value, from the ground and sky, to our hearts and minds. Do you think everyone who benefits is totally aware of that?

A person's upbringing may easily make a person believe this is all just the natural state of the world, but it is not. It is the reality we have created as a species; our "meaning." It is our product as a living factory. True, one's perspective can easily be that a factory is natural. We are of the earth and what we create is just as much so. The universe, however, is a place so unconcerned with humans and our "perspective," "meaning" and "reality," that it can be easy to forget that "natural" is something we made up to describe what "just happens."

Thing is, in a world run by beings of perspective, nothing really "just happens." What we call "reality" amounts to a living painting, an ongoing interpretation created by our brains using information we gather from organs and nerves relaying signals. Little electric pulses are always indicating absorption of radiation and pressure and we're continually rendering a composition for an audience of one.

Our ongoing grasp on "reality" is determined by a recollection system that's constantly in flux, rewriting information as it recalls, making memories of recalling memories, losing track and creating inconsistencies. Everything about our perception, recollection, interpretation, and output of all information is, *in every possible sense of the term*, imperfect.

Sure, there is something resembling what we describe as "universal fact," but it exists outside of human perception and operates outside of human parameters. It's also not *called* "universal fact;" this is a human term. It's not called a term at all. "Term" is a human term, too. It *just is*, and that's impossible for us to fully grasp, regardless of whether we think we can.

We must understand that *everything, as humans perceive it, genuinely isn't objective*. In his *Inaugural Dissertation, On the Form and Principles of the Sensible and Intelligible World*, philosopher Immanuel Kant theorizes that the hard boundary of the human mind is the human senses. He put forth the idea that we do not experience any actual object itself, but rather how our senses interact with it.

We all have varying strengths and weaknesses of sense, thus what we perceive is somewhat different. A time and place where we aren't all defining our own realities *hasn't happened*—nor can it. The things we have considered universal in the past change when we regard them with skepticism. Often, they outright crumble. The only possible reason anyone could even regard an object or observation as objective or universal is because they are not applying enough scrutiny to it. The less specific one's observations are, the less consistent with another person's view an object might be.

Sadly, when people take the step of applying skepticism and constants are found, they have a decent chance of being shunned. If it's contradictory to what we think now, it's dangerous to *who we are now*. Remember that "the customer is always right." Because we are asked to look at everything as a transaction in a neoliberal capitalist environment, we are to behave as a customer. This means that in everything from our language to what we expect to get out of friendships and jobs, we are meant to consider what we are buying. Was this a decent transaction? Please rate the seller.

If we're not right, we're wrong. If we're wrong, we're unemployable. If we can't make money, we can't eat. Significantly less can we buy merch or attend events. In today's situation, human needs of sustenance, community and identity *depend on our ability to spend*. Our ability to spend depends on our ability to seem right, so our ability to seem to be right becomes a priority. We have no real choice because we don't have access to all the information, thus we dig our heels in and develop identity around our beliefs. Then we must consume more validating products, services and content. The cycle continues in a hundred different directions and we're not supposed to comprehend it. It is amorphous and difficult to keep track of.

It may well be that some of the architects of this situation didn't understand what they were doing, either.

However, some did. People like Edward Bernays understood what things were and sought to use this knowledge, developing ideas and techniques that carried out these specific goals. However, it ultimately doesn't matter which motives led people to create and exploit this system; the system exists one way or another. It's there regardless of whether it's intentional or not. It's there whether crackpots are right about the illuminati or not. The goddamn lizards will be there, either literally or metaphorically, until something changes.

You and I can't fix these systemic problems ourselves. However, we can strive to minimize their effects in our own reality. This is not insignificant, though, as any system designed to control people is a tacit admission that people are powerful, and as people understand this, that power can be collectivized. I'd even argue that the reality we all see can't resemble what we call "factual" without doing so.

At our most basic level, you and I *must* acknowledge reality as *both the flaw and the strength* of humanity. It is our "meaning," our "product," and it isn't perfect at all. It is like all other human things; it can be garbage, or it can be amazing. That depends very much on what we decide it to be. Why should a small, rich group of assholes be the ones who get to determine what is real?

If two people observe the same thing and agree on what they saw, that doesn't make the thing objectively *exactly that*. Further, if two people disagree on it, whether explicitly or implicitly, we have the basis for artistic interpretation. Art isn't automatically amazing, but the potential is endless.

If the full population of the world accepted all the same contentions and evidence, it would result in a unanimous reality. We shouldn't assume this will ever happen, though, as it demands uniformity. It would demand perception as an objective phenomenon, which it isn't. Also, everyone simply agreeing doesn't mean the evidence is sound. The argument to the majority is fallacious; just because a ton of people say something doesn't make it objectively true.

So, what does? Well… nothing. Nothing human has been or ever will be just plain true.

This can be a blow to the psyche. It can feel like a major loss because when we examine this a little deeper, we find that we may just not have control of our surroundings in the way we think we do. It may even be necessary to traverse the stages of grief. If that's the road we end up taking, we *must* make it to the stage of acceptance. If we can get over the loss of objective reality, we may "lose" a perceived mastery over the material world and the knowledge "objective" examinations can yield; but the key word there is "perceived." It's not something we have ever had.

Now, that doesn't mean you go out and "live off the grid" in a hut somewhere in the temperate forests of Canada, as Wolverine did in certain stories. That's going to make your existence harder and will do nothing to change the overall situation. You're going to need to keep your job until no one needs a job. You're going to need to rent your home until there are no landlords. You're going to have to pay your mortgage and utility bills until a home and the services that make it habitable have all become a right. You're going to have to use and save money *until you don't.*

But you don't have to just sit and wait. This is the strength of the individual: at any time, you can say "fuck this."

You aren't looking out at the same reality as anyone else. All things in the world are not yours, but how you see such things is up to you. You must own this. Embrace it. We must make this weakness into a strength by understanding that the problem of reality is that there is no reality if *you* don't exist.

You probably care a great deal about the idea of "facts" or what's "real." I know I do. It matters on such a high level to me that I am using my reality trying to get others to see theirs for what it is: either a means of control you remain unaware of, as it exerts itself on you, or a means to build a world that is fair and rooted in evidence.

"Facts," currently, are what authorities have deemed the best explanation for our perception. This is both a good thing and a bad thing. As far as science goes, it's good that experts have a say in what is accepted as legitimate. The problem is, this is establishing a vertical, unquestionable hierarchy. Yes, someone who *lives* science—reads, experiments, publishes, etc.—should be regarded as worth listening to about science. But should they be given *power* over others? I don't really think so. This is one of the contradictions I don't know that we have a perfect resolution to, and thus should lean further into rather than recoil from.

I'm inclined to agree when folks say that authority is a corrupting force, too. I also think that the Religion of Me preys upon this perfectly legitimate concern, setting us up to live in our own custom realities by repeatedly indulging this flaw with conspiracy theories and outright false information presented as an explanation for unjust authority exercising power.

If you have addressed this conflict, you're on the path I hope you will continue to follow. I'll try to illuminate what I think that path looks like just a little more for you, but ultimately the best thing you can do to combat this as an individual is understand the system, the motives behind it, and talking to new people about it as much as you can. Even if *you* don't know what to do, eventually *we* will. The reason for that is that *we* can. *We* are capable of much more than *you or me*.

Somewhere you've likely heard the phrase "they own you." It might sound ridiculous, because you might feel like you are truly in charge of your life. You might feel powerful. Hell, you might *be* powerful in certain contexts. One of the things that compounds our ability to address the power structure is that even the oppressed might be slightly less oppressed than someone else and therefore have the capability to oppress them. Often, what happens *directly to us* seems more real than what does not. This is, again, The Religion of Me. Individualism is amazing at giving us an inch with the intent of making us *feel* like we got a mile.

The thing is, no one needs to own you in 2018. No one needs to care about you at all. No one even needs to think about you. An entity wishing to exert power over others simply needs to own the environment. Someone who owns the environment can engineer people's actions and consent by changing their circumstances. They not only do this; they are very good at it.

You don't have to have any idea who "they" are, you just must know how the power structure works. I would even argue that finding out everything about who "they" are is a distraction. Do we really need a dossier on everyone who is using the system? I do not. All that really matters is that large entities and wealthy individuals have actual goals of consolidating their power and work on a constant basis to do so. This is why we have five media companies owning the vast majority of the media. This is why you live near a Walmart.

That Walmart has been there a long time. At this point, you have accepted the idea of living near it as normal, because every time you've seen it, it's grabbed your attention. In maintaining some level of attention, there is no question anymore; Walmart is normal. "Normal" is a commodity because it is an idea.

You, as an individual, must find others. You must find out their problems, and offer them more than sympathy. You must take their problems seriously. I don't care how absurd they sound to you, they have a root somewhere. People do not need the idea that they have problems to be debunked. We need to collaborate on solutions.

That might mean finding the roots of problems that are very uncomfortable—problems where people who don't deserve blame are given it. It might mean changing assertions, and that very well may result in disagreement. That will require patience. It may even require you to go down rabbit holes which you don't agree with, even if only to prove something incorrect and to find a more productive mode of operation. You may fail. That's okay, because the greatest teacher... failure is.

If the commitment you are making is towards creating a workable, evidence-based collective reality, it means ending the need to be validated by capital and the systems it has created to uphold its interests. Unfortunately, that means an extremely difficult battle against the feeling of validation. You will be validated as you prove or uncover things and, frankly, you should. Feeling proud when one accomplishes something is not bad, but validation cannot become a thrill to seek, as capital will supply where there is demand. That's what has led us to a situation in which whatever we believe, someone seeking profit will ensure we are validated for it.

We should enjoy when we are proven right; it's just that being proven wrong is something we should maybe enjoy, too. Being wrong is not a flaw; it is a step.

We have a lot of steps to take and the walk is going to be long and painful. Most of these steps, we don't yet know (or have a full adaptation of lots of theoretical ideas for post-internet times). So much of what we use to survive today will be put into question tomorrow. A lot of what we personally subsist on is predicated on our acceptance of an environment that is intentionally curated to produce certain results. As we reject that mode of operation, much of the world will seem significantly less pleasant.

Hope does not require comfort. Though hope itself can be co-opted, that the future *can* become better is the only reason it ever *will*. Similarly, reality requires care, which requires conscious effort. Hollow weights take less effort to lift, so we must fill them with substance.

To seize yourself means to be hopeful, to enjoy things *for yourself*, to be critical of those things and all things you perceive. Since we must do things that serve the interests of capital to survive, we must do it with the understanding power is being exerted over us. Be open, but be careful. Don't needlessly make enemies because you're woke and they're money; endlessly make friends because friends are great. Understand why things happen in this world and you'll get what we're up against.

What is your perspective on "revolution?" I used quotation marks again, so I'd bet you know that I have one. Revolution is a word. Words are human creations. It means something, but that meaning came from people. Revolution, to me, means a total systemic change. That, itself, can mean a million different things; it can be violent or non-violent, political or even emotional. Whatever form it takes, though. I believe it must be as close to the will of all people as it can be. It must be owned and operated by the public. That is what I think is missing from many calls for revolution in the world of today; for those calling hardest, revolution is the goal. It can't be.

Revolution is a means... to what? My hope is in fairness and equity. I can't guarantee that yours is, too. Even if it is, we can't just believe in it; we have to face reality. What do we agree these things mean? What don't we?

Customizing reality is something every single one of us is going to do for the rest of our lives. We are groomed to do it in a way that keeps the heat off the people at the top. There's a dependency on the hierarchy that is nurtured, keeping everything real.

But it's stopped seeming real, hasn't it?

PETER COFFIN

ABOUT THE AUTHOR

Peter Coffin is *basically* a satirist and *more or less* a cultural critic in a variety of mediums. Besides this book, he produces the video series "Very Important Documentaries" and "Many Peters," and a TV commercial criticism show, "ADVERSARIES." He also writes "about the author" sections, but mainly in other people's books. Not this book.

twitter.com/petercoffin
youtube.com/petercoffin

68832534R00119

Made in the USA
Middletown, DE
02 April 2018